DISCOVERING
your
GOD
SELF

The Incredible Secrets of Your Spiritual Nature Revealed

BRUCE BERNSTEIN

BLB Consulting, Inc.
1625 Mid Valley Dr, Ste 1-1022
Steamboat Springs, CO 80487

First e-Publication Date: 2021
First Print Publication Date: 2021
ISBN eBook/Digital Versions: 978-0-9861533-4-1
ISBN Paperback Version: 978-0-9861533-5-8

ATTENTION CORPORATIONS, UNIVERSITIES, COLLEGES, OTHER EDUCATIONAL, PROFESSIONAL, AND RELIGIOUS ORGANIZATIONS: Quantity discounts are available on bulk purchases of this book for educational and gift purposes, or as premiums (premiums must be approved by both the author and publisher). For details, contact the publisher at the address above.

For more information about other books and online courses and classes from Bruce Bernstein, please visit: www.BruceBernstein.me

This book is dedicated to all those still mired in the illusion of temporary and artificial highs and lows; the sleepers yet to awaken, who substitute fleeting moments of elation and disappointment, success and failure, lust and anger, for the actual happiness quietly waiting beneath those distractions to be uncovered and acknowledged. It is my desire to light their path to conscious living and an awakening to the more comfortable, content, and joyful reality they will find.

"Things can be easy for us, or they can be hard. We can make good decisions and we can make bad ones. We can have a life that is filled with more joy, or a life of constant struggle, disappointment, and sadness. All this is up to us. Our experiences and results are simply outcomes of the decisions we make. So, it only makes sense to become aware of your inner motivations, to understand the cogs that turn beneath the surface and how these actively shape and determine your choices."

— **BRUCE BERNSTEIN**

THANK YOU

As a thank you for reading this book, and to give you an extra push along your path of discovery and inner awareness, I created a few videos to light your way. These contain some very effective techniques I have successfully used during meditation. Please access these videos here:

WWW.BRUCEBERNSTEIN.ME/EXTRAS-DISCOVERING-YOUR-GOD-SELF/

Discovering Your God Self
Calibrated Level of Consciousness:

For those familiar with Dr. David R. Hawkins, MD, PhD and his work calibrating levels of consciousness, the calibrated level of consciousness for this book: 856

CONTENTS

WHAT TO EXPECT

"Heaven is not a country or a continent, it is a state, a condition within oneself, only experienced when the rhythm is in perfect working order. If one knows this one realizes that happiness is man's own property. Man is his own enemy; he seeks for happiness in the wrong direction and never finds it. It is a continual illusion. Man thinks, 'If I had this or that I should be happy for ever,' and he never arrives at it because he pursues an illusion instead of the truth. Happiness is only to be found within, and when man tunes himself he finds everything which his soul yearns for within himself." [1]

B ased on the fact that you've opened this book and begun reading, I surmise that, at some level, you are searching. You've come to a fork in the road and chosen the path of promise. Welcome!

---

[1]   Hazrat Inayat Khan, Wahiduddin's Web, The Spiritual Message of Hazrat Inayat Khan, Volume XIV — The Smiling Forehead Part II — The Deeper Side of Life, Chapter XXI Divine Impulse, https://wahiduddin.net/mv2/XIV/XIV_2_21.htm

If you're anything like me, or the way I used to be, you may have found yourself sucked into the Spiritual vacuum our world has become, filled with endless newsfeeds, distractions, anxieties, and unsatisfying social interactions, and have realized that there must be more to this life. You'd like to find a deeper understanding and meaning to truly ground yourself and experience greater joy and purpose.

Thank you for choosing this little book. I wrote *Discovering Your God Self... The Incredible Secrets of Your Spiritual Nature Revealed* to fill a knowledge gap. This gap is a source of misunderstanding that has created much of our individual and collective anger, hate, injustice, disappointment, mistrust, and the other negativities in our lives. It is my hope that you will find value herein and use it to create a more fulfilling, wonderful, and joyful life for yourself and, in turn, allow your newfound Spirituality to shine brightly and influence our world.

This is not the beginning of your journey and it certainly will not be the end. Your journey likely began thousands of years ago, perhaps even millions or billions of years ago, depending on when your soul first came to be. It will continue long after you finish this book, even if you reject all its ideas, and long after your body dies.

I am thrilled to have the opportunity to provide information you may not know consciously, and might never have considered, but which is the foundation for everything you are, have done, and will do in your life. In this book, you will discover your God Self, the actual God essence that is you, along with its different components.

You may be wondering — and I hope you are — what I mean when I use the phrase "your God Self." *Your* God Self is different from *mine*. It is unique, yet also the same, part of the bigger whole. I know it sounds counterintuitive, and it may not make sense to you just yet, but you will understand by the end of this book.

As you read, please keep in mind that this book is not about religion. It does, however, contain information I believe all religions *should* teach. The information I've presented can, and should, be incorporated into every religious practice, or it can replace organized religion entirely, as many of the great Spiritual teachers and masters have encouraged. *Discovering Your God Self . . . The Incredible Secrets of Your Spiritual Nature Revealed* explains the concept of God on a deeply personal level, a God that is free from the clutches, reinterpretation, and distortion often imposed consciously or unconsciously by organizations and institutions.

You will discover and understand how God is everything, with no exceptions. Just as trillions of water molecules combine to form the oceans, there is a piece of God within you that is separate, yet also the same, as the God within me. This is why all the great masters throughout history have suggested that we look inside ourselves (internal) rather than to the world (external) for Spiritual answers. In fact, there are trillions of individual pieces of this God, and they are found in every living organism — fungi, bacteria, fish, animals, insects, and more. Each may take a different form, but all are part of the same source: the Greater God.

The body itself has often been referred to as the temple of God. This is because God lives inside your body. In other words, you are a manifestation of God housed within walls of flesh, which uses your body as a tool to experience physical existence. Within you lives a singular and unique piece of this magnificent and enormous essence.

The God within you has several components, all of which will be explored in this book. You will discover concepts, ideas, and truths that will apply to every aspect of your life. They will be fundamentally useful for anyone who becomes aware of these facets of our internal world and employs this extraordinary power to transform themselves.

The time has come to bring the ancient knowledge that lies dormant in the depths of your being back to conscious awareness, to incorporate it into our modern, fast-paced world.

Long ago, before exciting advances in transportation and technology began shrinking our world, the slower-paced and quieter routines made it easier to incorporate this essential Spiritual information into daily life. In our world today, there are so many distractions which, like a fishing lure, are bright shiny objects (flashes of light or sound from our smartphones, for example) competing for our attention. Although not innately bad, these have conspired to hide vital information from our awareness. How many times have you gone to your phone to quickly answer an important message and then found yourself mindlessly scrolling through social media and confronted by a host of opinions and advertisements? Are you aware that these things then occupied considerable space in your head and may have devalued and distracted you from the reality of your current life experience? This happens everywhere in our modern world — it is cross-cultural and international.

But there is hope.

We can change this trend by returning to our Inner Selves and making more conscious choices that enable us to stride down the path of real and active change. When we do this as individuals it can set off a chain reaction. We first affect our own lives which then can influence our families and friends. Then it can filter out to communities, the world, and the next generations. You don't just owe it to yourself to discover your God Self, you owe it to every living thing that existed before, during, and will come after your life.

In *Discovering Your God Self... The Incredible Secrets of Your Spiritual Nature Revealed*, I have presented information in a way that is both meaningful and user-friendly, to borrow (ahem, steal) a term from our modern-day world. I wrote this book to help people understand that there is more to life than meets the eye and that there is more to us humans than many of us will ever know.

The information presented in this book will allow you to transform yourself by giving you a deeper knowledge of ancient Spiritual teachings. Information and knowledge are only a jumping-off point. Wisdom is the end game. Knowledge can be obtained through study. Wisdom is only acquired through experience. (Please note: I capitalize the words Spiritual and Spirituality throughout this book, as I use these words as names of the concept of our Inner Selves. As with the name "God," I believe they should be capitalized.) Ultimately, how you interpret Spirituality is your choice. You can choose to accept (some or all) the information I present to you and use it to transform your life, or you can discard it and carve your own path. Either way, know that you are loved, appreciated, and are an equal part of the greater whole.

The power is in your hands.

Any transformation requires willingness, bravery, and attention (especially to life's smaller details). Are you comfortable stepping into the unknown to discover lost wisdom that will benefit your life and others around you?

When molding a lump of clay, the attention is on the outside to form it to one's vision. Similarly, we can mold our inner processes to bring the power and potential of our Inner Selves to the forefront. Make no mistake, the power to create the life and lifestyle you desire is within you. Reconnecting with your inner essence is one part of the equation to attain the true freedom, success, and love you desire. We all desire these comforts; we want to experience the best life has to offer. I'd go as far as saying that experience is the essence of life, so why not experience the things we genuinely want, rather than being victimized by life's circumstances?

One word you might use to describe the inner essence I'm discussing would be "soul," a term I've decided to use sparingly in this book. That's mainly because the term is loaded — it has been misused and misunderstood over the millennia. In place of "soul," we are referring to the exploration of the individual components of you, also known as your Inner Selves. These Inner Selves are the real Spiritual you, the entire you, and they can be used by you to manifest the world of your dreams. And, as more individuals choose to Spiritually transform, the more our dear Earth can be molded into the heavenly place most desire it to be.

I came to the conclusions I will share with you through many years of self-exploration — a deep introspective study of my Inner Selves. I was led to these conclusions, sometimes against my will. But despite my Ego self, which often screamed, kicked, and made unnecessary demands like a red-faced child desiring ice cream before dinner, I persevered. It doesn't have to be that harsh for you.

Sure, I studied the writings of several masters I'd been guided to and which resonated with me, including Buddha, Jesus, Yogananda, and Dr. David R. Hawkins. (I recommend you use this approach, too. Use your inner guidance as best as you can to find materials that will help you, an approach which may have led you to this book in the first place.) However, wisdom is not gained through the study and knowledge of things. This was a tough lesson for me as, by nature, I'm a left-brained (analytical, methodical) individual. Real wisdom is only acquired experientially; it comes from within. It is less of a process of *adding* and more one of *uncovering* what's always been there. Remove the debris to find what's hidden beneath.

Ultimately, discovering wisdom and reaching higher levels of consciousness are not entirely intellectual pursuits. They're mostly found through feeling the Inner Selves, which is why it is valuable — critical — to know what's truly inside of us.

My journey to Spiritual reawakening and understanding began in the mid-1980s and continues to this day. The more I learn, the more I realize I do not know. The more I realize I do not know, the more I persist in my search for answers. The learning never ends.

Life is a continual learning process — the mastery of each lesson will lead to more questions than answers. Always ask questions and challenge things that don't feel right and build on your knowledge and wisdom from there.

Complacency leads to stagnation. Stagnation tends to create a flock of people who are so desperate for meaning they'll follow any leader who makes them feel better about themselves. Consider what happened in Germany in the 1920s and 1930s when the country was suffering from emotional, Spiritual, and financial stagnation. The people elected one of the most destructive leaders in human history. The problem is that the flock is always subject to misinformation and being misled. Remember that stagnation is contrary to the universe, which is in a constant state of change (flux). Keep this in mind and apply it as a foundational model so you, too, will benefit from continual change.

Regardless of beliefs, religious practice, or a lack thereof, the path for all is one of Spiritual awareness and increasing levels of consciousness. Wherever you are on your path of Spiritual discovery — a beginner just starting out, or at a more advanced level — I sincerely hope you enjoy this book and find it useful.

Always move forward. Stay in the present and try to remain conscious of your Inner Selves. Strive to create awareness and balance yourself between your inner world and the outer world. Use each moment to advance your life and increase your consciousness. Higher Spiritual awareness will bring the inner peace all seek, as well as a more rewarding and successful outer world experience.

Again… Welcome. The incredible secrets of your Spiritual nature are about to be Revealed. I hope you are ready to discover your God Self.

INTRODUCTION

Spirituality is often misunderstood. It is frequently confused with religion and wrongly identified with psychics, crystals, and even meditation. None of these, including some of the so-called "Western" religions, are necessarily about Spirituality. Certainly, Spirituality may have been the initial purpose of these religions, but the focus for many (perhaps even most) is not about teaching what you are about to learn, which is the foundation of Spirituality. There are religions, sects, and denominations whose particular practices and teachings are still closely aligned with Spirituality. Others, though, not so much.

So far, after reading just one paragraph of this chapter, you may already be thinking that I'm crazy for even suggesting that religion is not about Spirituality. The good news is I'm not crazy (at least, I don't think I am!), I'm just observing the way religions have evolved.

Let me explain. It is true that some religions contain *elements* of Spirituality. Others, though, have eliminated it entirely from their everyday teachings. The reasons for this are outside the scope of this book, but I find it important to mention that we now find ourselves in a situation where religion and honest-to-goodness Spirituality are not the same. In some cases, they're not even in the same ballpark.

Often, religions concern themselves with ritual, or they ask entire congregations to repeat pre-scripted offerings or prayers. They appear more eager to promote community activities and charity (which are of high value in themselves) over the truths found in the teachings of personal Spirituality. Typically, their failings reside in neglecting to teach the essential information about the *Inner Selves*. This is a problem because the study of the Inner Selves is the essence of Spirituality. Many religions have fallen into the practice of conflating Spirituality with morality, which are not the same thing.

Spirituality is all about the knowledge and continual awareness of the Inner Selves, how they interact with one another, and how to use them to be a creator and to create the life of one's dreams. The "Inner Selves" is often referred to as the soul, and that's the primary focus of this book. When you've finished reading it, you will understand all the aspects of your Inner Selves. Religion has been given an ample opportunity — thousands of years, in fact — to share this vital information and to positively impact the world and people's lives. I encourage you to honestly examine the world around you. Given our collective history and the current state of the world, has religion *really* been effective?

Our world is suffering from an increasing level of inequality and chaos, with demagogues taking power and actively working to deprive or hurt the majority to benefit the few. Wars are waged continuously. Real problems with our environment and climate are given lip-service or their existence as issues are completely denied. Population growth has exceeded the planet's capacity to adequately sustain human life comfortably over the long term, and our population is still increasing. We are close to running out of natural resources that currently afford us our comfortable lives. On top of all this, at the time of writing, the world is embroiled in the COVID-19 pandemic.

Could all these be symptoms of a bigger, more internal problem we have with ourselves?

What we see in the outer world are manifestations based on the state of humankind's inner world — its consciousness. These are mere reflections, a mirror image, of humankind's deepest, often hidden, fears. For many, life's trials and tribulations are difficult to navigate. If the timeline reported by climate science is correct — and I have no reason to doubt it — life could become even more precarious sooner than many realize. But there's good news. The world is ready for a shift in consciousness. This shift will be fundamental to human survival, both physical and Spiritual. Our survival depends on it and you are essential to this shift.

Each day, more people are coming to the realization that something is missing in their lives, even if they cannot yet define it. I'd argue it's because most people are not yet acquainted with their Inner Selves. We don't yet fully understand our true nature, the reality of who and what we are, or the real, innate power we each have immediately at our disposal. Too many of us don't know even the most basic information: where to look for assistance and answers, and how to begin helping ourselves. This book will give you a more complete understanding of yourself through the lens of your Inner Selves.

People are increasingly searching for better information and practical, actionable answers to life's most pressing questions. We have a whole universe of knowledge at our fingertips due to smartphones and the internet, yet this source is also jam-packed with distractions and misinformation. And religions cannot give us all these answers. Even if they do, they're usually obscured by misinterpreted allegories, metaphors, or moralistic and sometimes self-servingly false lectures or presentations labeled as sermons.

Answers can be found in real Spirituality. But it is up to each of us to discover and follow our own path. Those who take the time to discover their true Spiritual nature, in an honest and diligent way, will end up in a state of transcendence that is universal, that anyone who experiences will find themselves in the same place, with the same answers, even if these answers come in slightly different forms or flavors. The basic understanding and realizations will be the same. This is the power of the God Self and its hidden secrets. You already have the basic understanding and answers within and these remain the same no matter who you are — rich or poor, tall or short, introverted or extroverted.

This short book offers you a deep dive into the powerful realm of Spirituality, and will provide you with practical, straightforward, and foundational information that you can use to ascend the ladder of consciousness. No matter where you are on the ladder right now, this book has something for you. Although a mere introduction to a Spiritual life's principal elements, the concepts and ideas revealed throughout these pages should be known to everyone, regardless of religious beliefs or even their level of interest in Spirituality. In time, you will discover information here that has the potential to make formal, organized religious practice less relevant, less important. That's okay. Religion is not a prerequisite for a better life or to enter heaven. For those who are not at all religious, this book will provide something that is universal and separate from that. For those who are religious, this book will add to and enhance the foundation of your beliefs.

Some will find that the things contained in this book will enable significant and beneficial changes to their lives and level of consciousness. Along the way, please realize that any transformational journey like this may initially create confusion and perhaps even some negative emotions and experiences. This is normal and would likely be one of your Inner Selves rebelling against a change in the status quo, or a string of events ultimately intended to facilitate the changes you desire.

Some questions you may have asked yourself are *So, who am I? What do I know about Spirituality?* These are good questions. Only you can know the answers, but one thing I can tell you is this:

Skepticism and asking questions are fundamental to Spirituality, as this will bring you closer to the truth.

Or, in short: question everything, including what I've written in this book.

A word of caution, though; too much skepticism is not a good thing. It can delay your learning which, in turn, will delay your advancement to the higher levels of consciousness. Admittedly, I could be the poster child for that approach. I am a natural-born skeptic, often to my own detriment. This is due to one of my core issues in this lifetime: trust. The Spiritual understanding that I share with you now was a struggle for me to attain, and probably more of a struggle than it would be for many. I had to win hard-fought battles for the wisdom and spiritual knowledge I have gained. But I'm glad I fought those battles. They brought understanding, peace, happiness, love, and better health.

I learned early along my path that change is constant. Nothing is static. The universe and consciousness are dynamic and reflect this truth. Knowing this has kept me interested and open to learning new things. However, I still find Spiritual change and growth difficult — the rebellious nature of one of my Inner Selves is always trying to undo the good work I've done!

Although it took me a long time to accept my destiny, it is now apparent that I was intended to teach these truths to others. To learn, though, experiences are often dual in nature. As one force within pushed me to dive even deeper, another objected. The duality within is always there. The objector usually was a particular inner aspect of me (one of my Inner Selves) who likes throwing tantrums and made my learning difficult, but also extensive. To teach something well, one must first develop a strong understanding of the subject matter. So, for me, learning was meant to be difficult. Difficulty is the best way for me to learn (as it keeps things interesting, and I can be skeptically stubborn) and it was the price I had to pay to fulfill my obligation and inner desire to teach this material to others. I have come to realize that the obligation to teach this was something I'd agreed to do before being born into this life. Had things come too easily for me, I would not have been able to provide the detailed explanations and information you will find as you continue reading.

Your path to understanding doesn't have to be as difficult as mine, but I'm not saying that yours will be easy, either. We all tend to make things more complex than they need to be. So, I'm here to simplify!

As you read further, I encourage you to keep an open heart and mind. Become aware of your deepest, innermost feelings — a topic I will discuss thoroughly in future chapters. And, if you experience a feeling in your gut that something just feels right, accept it. Fighting your gut instincts will only delay your learning and the benefits that acquiring new wisdom will bring. You are in control, always, and can revisit your choice at any time. With that in mind, after choosing to accept the information you've read herein, and given it time to filter into your consciousness, if you realize you're not comfortable with it you can discard it, unlearn it, and move forward with something else.

An open heart and mind will help both skeptics and non-skeptics better understand and incorporate into their lives the ideas presented in this book, and will help fill the hole many feel within. This is the ladder to greater success, happiness, and love. Each rung on the ladder of Spirituality will lead us to the next stage of higher consciousness.

1

Unmasking Reality

As I write this chapter, it is Friday, January 31, 2020, about 11:15 in the morning, Eastern Time, in the United States of America. The world financial markets are under considerable downward pressure today as they have been for the last few days. The reason? Fear. The world is reacting to a potential pandemic, a new and potentially lethal coronavirus: COVID-19. (Not too long after the day I wrote this paragraph, COVID-19 was officially declared a pandemic.)

COVID-19 originated in Wuhan, China, in a country where overpopulation has long been a problem. It has been such a significant problem that back in the 1960s and 1970s, the Chinese government instituted a one child policy, limiting the number of offspring per family to just one. Economic sanctions, forced sterilizations, and mandatory abortions were just some of the punishments dished out by the Chinese government for those who failed to adhere to the policy. While the policy was absurd, especially to anyone outside of China (and plenty who lived in the country), and while it was a blatant infringement of human rights, it also was an (ethically questionable) acknowledgement of a very real problem: overpopulation. China's population was so large (it still is the country with the largest population, with just under 1.5 billion inhabitants at the time of writing) that the government tried to implement a solution. Now the whole world is becoming so densely populated that, soon enough, there will be far too many people for the planet to cope with. The question we must answer is: what can we do about it? (Please stay with me. This is not a political discussion. It directly relates to Spirituality.)

Since the 1970s, the world's population has just about doubled, from about 3.686 billion in 1970, to about 7.7 billion in 2019. At that rate, the population of the world is projected to grow to approximately 9.8 billion by 2050, which, according to at least one sociobiologist and Harvard professor, Edward O. Wilson, is the limit of Earth's capacity to comfortably support human life.

The problems overpopulation present are already manifesting. The earth and its available resources are approaching limits from which there might be no return. Add to this the associated rise in sea level — which threatens the lives and lifestyles of many, potentially engulfing entire countries — and we're presented with the possibility of a very bleak future if we do not raise our collective consciousness and intervene. One of the problems of overpopulation is the excess pollution created by all people living today, especially those living in the developed world. The equation is simple:

more people = more vehicles = higher carbon emissions, as well as more refuse. We also must consider possible consequence of an undersupply of food, drinking water, land, and open spaces. Naturally, the increase in carbon emissions contribute to climate change, which in turn causes rising sea levels, which will overtake some of the lands where people live, grow food, and recreate. The problem is compounding, and as time goes on, unless changes are made, the issue will only become more urgent.

While these realizations seem obvious, the overpopulation issue has yet to be openly and honestly debated. Religion has played a significant part in that, discouraging birth control and encouraging large families, as have individual desires to *feel* happy, believing that having many children would lead to that by filling the emptiness that many experience.

The COVID-19 pandemic has rattled people. Predictably, the burgeoning Earthly population and ease of world travel were both factors in COVID-19's rapid spread. Time will tell if we can reverse this trend and defeat it with the application of proper scientific analysis and solutions. This threat is pushing all our buttons, and we are awakening to the delicate balance between continued human existence, and extinction.

The determining factor — the trail that will lead us to better choices — lies within each one of us. How did we reach this point? We lost our way. We've lost touch with who we are, with the ultimate reality or our true Spiritual nature. We've forgotten and even actively ignored our Inner Selves. The time has come for us to awaken from our collective slumber.

We are a walking paradox, connected to the whole world via the internet but also truly disconnected from everything we are. Part of this disconnect is due to the reliance we've placed on religion, with the hope that it would offer us the correct guidance and teaching. The one thing religions should be addressing right now, and aren't, is the true nature of Spirituality. This deficiency is likely caused by a mixture of two factors: innocent error and intentional deception. Religions have lost sight of their true purpose and transformative potential. They should help people connect with and remain connected to their Inner Selves. For the most part, they do neither.

It is no accident that I use the plural term "Selves" to describe our innate nature as humans. It is deliberate and accurately reflects reality. Our physicality aside, there are five principal aspects to our humanness that all people need to know, regardless of their religious beliefs, motivations, or Spiritual intentions. Knowing and understanding these five things will automatically begin the process of raising one's individual level of consciousness as well as that of the world-at-large.

Once consciousness has begun to raise, different and more beneficial choices will be made and the problems in our own lives will begin to resolve. These changes will then spill over to the problems we see globally. Improvements will ensue naturally.

I've teased you enough. Let's get to these five principal aspects of Self:

1. **The Individualized Self**

   » This is the part that you identify as 'you.'

2. **The Communicator**

   » A barrier to keep the Individualized Self and the God Self separate, but also allows for communication between the two, mostly from the Individualized Self to the God Self.

3. **The God Self**

   » Your individual and unique piece of the Greater God.

These are the three fundamental 'Selves,' but what about the other two?

This is where things can get a little messy, the source of much of our confusion. The Individualized Self is made up of two critical components. These two operate beneath the surface of our awareness until we choose to raise our consciousness and bring their influencing energies and existence to the fore. They are simultaneously the source of our happiness, but also our disappointments, and are the foundation of all the world's problems. They are:

4. The Ego self

> » This is the fear-based aspect of you.
>
> *Please Note: Throughout this book, I have used a lower case 's' for the word 'self' in Ego self. This is deliberate and was done to draw attention to the fact that the Ego self is an illusion, a false representation of self.*

5. The True Self

> » This is the Love-based aspect of you. (All our emotions are expressions of either Love or fear.)

Simple math: the former three plus the latter two equals five. (Even as a young child, I was good at math!) Since the latter two are so complex, and absolutely critical to all aspects of our lives, I consider them to be main components even though they are only parts of something bigger — the Individualized Self.

The above information is the golden key to your goodness and happiness and is the foundation of Spirituality and your Spiritual nature. This is what everyone needs to know, understand, and incorporate into daily life. **This is the *soul*.**

These five factors need to be properly accounted for when considering all our tastes, preferences, and desires. They are the factors in determining how our lives unfold — the experiences we have — and contribute to all the decisions we make, including the question of having children and overpopulation. The choice to have children, and how many to have, is greatly influenced by these inner aspects. Most are unaware of this dynamic, which relates to all aspects of your life and which you will learn more in the coming chapters. To complete the circle on the issue of overpopulation, the question that needs to be considered when making the choice to have children, and how many, as well as to all our choices, is: Which voice are you aligned with and responding to, the Ego self or the True Self? What is the internal motivating factor behind the choices you make?

So, knowing these five aspects of you — the Individualized Self, including the Ego self and the True Self, the Communicator, and the God Self — is the first critical piece of knowledge in your new journey. In the coming chapters, these will be discussed in greater detail. Before we get to this critical and powerful information, though, I have found that sharing this information usually brings out the same question: How did you learn this? I am going to answer this excellent question.

2

Wisdom Is Experiential

B ack around 1960, there lived a four-year-old boy. Despite his young age, he'd already begun pondering his existence and asking some of life's more challenging questions.

On the second level of a small, split-level home on Long Island in a middle-class suburb of New York City, the young boy sat on the carpet in the living room under the watchful eye of his mother, who had just sat down on the sofa. Making eye contact with his mother, he asked, "Where was I before I was born?" Startled, she looked around the living room, as if someone were going to answer for her. She had no idea what to say and remained silent for a moment before settling on a response.

"You just weren't," she finally responded, hoping to end the conversation before it really began. The boy considered the answer carefully, then said, "That's not right." His mother glared back at him, astonished.

If you haven't already guessed, that boy was me. Some sixty years later, my recollection of that conversation is not as vivid as it had once been, especially since I was such a young child when it happened. But the memory is real. This conversation took place. My mother confirmed this when we spoke about it later in life, when I was in my thirties. I knew even as a young child — and still know now — that there was more to life than what we can see, hear, feel, smell, and taste in our three-dimensional world.

During my early years, a gentle, soft, and loving inner voice — one not audible through the ears — would offer me guidance. I mostly heard it when I became frightened, but it spoke to me at other times too. For a young child, it seemed as though there was an endless supply of frightening things in this world, so this voice visited me frequently, each time offering supportive and loving advice. I often considered it my own personal defender; a comforting, reassuring third parent who included each new concern I presented on a growing list of things from which it would protect me, like diseases I learned about from doctor shows I saw on TV.

This inner guidance was with me until my early teens when puberty erupted and became a distracting force. At this point, as is the case for most, I became more concerned with my friends and "fitting in" than anything else. I was overly preoccupied with the world outside of myself, more focused on my image and all the other banal yet consuming things many pursue during adolescence. Sure, this is part of life's natural progression, but this commonality doesn't make the experience any less challenging. The outcome of this distraction, at least for me, was my disconnection from the soft voice and its loving guidance. Later in life,

I even questioned whether it had ever existed at all. Even worse, along with its disappearance also went any sense of inner comfort from its sympathetic words and advice. I'd come to expect this support, especially when I found life's adventure intimidating. I was left to rely on only my thoughts, comments from my peers, and my parent's well intentioned, but sometimes deficient ideas for comfort and guidance.

Both my parents had strong, left-brained (analytical) personalities. They were highly educated and intelligent people, so I often looked to them for answers. I placed them on pedestals and thought they knew everything. It wasn't until later in life that I realized, despite meaning well, my parent's answers and advice weren't always the best, at least for me.

I did well enough in high school and continued my education at a prestigious university. But I know I didn't apply myself to the best of my ability. I did not realize this at the time, but even then, I already was lost, travelling through life without a map. I was experiencing life on my own for the first time and focused on exploring that freedom more than I did my studies. So, while I did learn as a student, I didn't take full advantage of the opportunities that higher education offered. Looking back, it is apparent that I attended college before I was ready.

The rudderless life I'd been living continued into my late 20s. I had adopted the prevailing herd mentality of the times, which included the notion that a good job, a decent apartment, and an active social life were the key elements to happiness, and it worked... for a while. I believed that I was happy, but I wasn't. *Thinking* you're happy and *being* happy are vastly different things. Sure, I laughed with friends, looked forward to hanging out and partying, and I was good at my job. It was only after something inside began reaching out to me that I then understood the full extent of my unhappiness. In fact, I was utterly miserable. I was uncomfortable in my own skin and also with life in general, unsure of my personality and my place in the world, disappointed in myself and the choices I was making, and frightened of spending time alone.

For too long, I had switched off my inner feelings just like so many people do when they step over the threshold into adulthood, and it never crossed my mind that I might not be happy, that there was something more to life that I wasn't experiencing. I had spent too much time focusing on the outer world, the rat race and the hustle and bustle of everyday life, and was neglecting my Inner Selves. My search for outer validation rather than inner experience was my own grand deception. I was unconscious, deluded by convictions of what I thought life should be, and struggled daily to understand the meaning and purpose of life. Why was I here? Why was I alone? How do I create happiness?

I asked myself a question, and I encourage you to ask yourself the same one: *Is life only about getting a job, making money, hanging out with friends, getting a house, getting married, and having a family?* I used to envision these things as markers of what success and happiness should look like. But it wasn't working for me. In fact, as much as I wanted it to work, this type of life never felt right to me. I ignored these doubts, though, and vigorously pursued it anyway. I was wandering the desert of delirium, looking for the promised land, but didn't have the faintest idea of what that land would look like. I followed the herd, trying to fit in, because I thought they had the answers, that they knew better than I did (as I'd erroneously believed about my parents). It was at this time when the seeds of my inner awareness began to sprout, which allowed the previously suppressed feeling of emptiness to emerge. This was an important first step, though I did not know it at the time. It was the seed that would soon germinate to a search for something better.

Then, in the mid-1980s, strange things began happening to me. However, because my perspective was so limited, I mostly ignored them; dismissed them as coincidental, bizarre, and unexplainable. I tried to conclude — or convinced myself to believe — that what I was experiencing was nothing more than a series of illusions, or even hallucinations, but they persisted.

One night, I was shocked out of a deep sleep by what I thought was a hard slap to my face. Once the fog of sleepiness disappeared, I still felt the sting of this "slap" lingering on my right cheek. I gently rubbed the stubble-covered area with my fingers. I looked around the small, darkened, one-room apartment. I saw no one. I was alone. I felt a wave of fear shudder through my body.

As disturbing as this was, I was able to fall asleep quickly afterward. I woke up the next day (a Saturday) and had an urge I'd not felt before. Without much deliberation, I got dressed and began walking my neighborhood. Before long, I found myself standing before a small, independent bookstore. Although I had lived in this neighborhood for about three years, this was the first time I had seen this shop. Like many retail stores in that old, East Village neighborhood in New York City, it was a few steps down from street level in a basement of a five story, walk-up apartment building, its aging red brick facade darkened by soot and other city created elements.

I went in and quickly realized that this was not the sort of bookstore I was used to visiting. It was different. I wasn't sure why I felt this way at first, but I was intrigued. A glance around the store revealed many interesting things: crystals, incense burning and for sale, books (of course), and other objects that might be considered "Spiritual." A section of books called out to me so I wandered over. As if by magic, I was drawn to a few in particular and pulled them from the shelves. I skimmed the titles and back covers.

Two of them excited me, so I bought them. One was about astral projection and the other about meditation. At the cash register, as I reached into my back pocket to grab my wallet, I saw a wooden carved sign behind the cashier, which made me realize that not only was this a metaphysical bookstore, but it also specialized in Wiccan materials. I must admit, that freaked me out a little, caught me unaware. I wasn't at all familiar with Wicca or Witchcraft and the books I chose were not about these subjects at all. The idea of Witchcraft felt too dark for me. However, I thanked the cashier, turned from her, smiled to myself, shook off my discomfort, and left the store.

I quickly read those two books. Considering I'd barely read any books at that time, this was a standout moment for me. I went from reading one book every five years to devouring two books in a week.

Each of the books contained information and ideas I had never come across before, but I had the feeling something had guided me towards them for a reason, even though I didn't know why. Looking back, it is now apparent that, for me, those books did exactly what they were intended to do. They were supposed to capture my imagination and put me on the path of truth so I could seek more. I was destined to learn about the intricacies and reality of our world and existence. Deep inside me, perhaps somewhere primal, something had awakened. It was a feeling of knowing, similar to the one I had as a four-year-old boy when I'd asked my mother difficult questions about life and our collective reality.

I've been learning ever since, studying many different philosophies, books, materials, and lectures. I have now become familiar with various subjects from many different perspectives including works about the Essenes, an ancient Jewish sect who raised Jesus when he was a child; and an interesting man named Sai Baba, a Spiritual master in India who performed little miracles daily for his devotees. About fifteen years later, I came upon another yogi from India, Paramahansa Yogananda, who had who immigrated to the US and created the Self Realization Fellowship. His books and other writings touched me on the deepest levels. At the end of one of his books, a free course was offered by mail. At that time, the internet was hardly booming, but I signed up and paid a small fee to learn more about his philosophy. Soon, I began getting monthly lessons by mail from his institution. It took me about two years to get through all the lessons.

During this time, I also discovered Dr. David R. Hawkins and began studying his books. He was a brilliant man, a world-renowned and successful psychiatrist who, even as a child, had what could be considered supernatural experiences. He was truly enlightened and wrote about enlightenment from his brilliant, scientific perspective. Because his books are filled with so much wisdom and were written at such a high intellectual level, reading them took a lot of energy and attention. These are not casual reads. Finishing them took time — many months and even more than a year for at least one. Despite their difficulty, I kept at it, not just reading but also studying, seeking every morsel of information and wisdom I could find.

Dr. Hawkins wrote to his intellectual capacities, which were considerable and, in my opinion, well above genius level. His books were certainly not written with the masses in mind. In fact, in at least one of his books, I remember him saying something along the lines of "you don't need to read my books — they aren't necessary for your growth." His philosophy centered on the duality within and he postulated that each person would eventually find their way to advanced consciousness regardless of what books they read. It was his belief that it might take many lifetimes. I read his books anyway — call me a rebel. I was eager to advance my Spiritual understanding and welcomed any help I could find.

To be honest, I disagree with Dr. Hawkins' notion that people will eventually find their way and that introducing them to new information is not necessary. I do agree with the underlying premise but believe that it is useful, if not critical that people have information so they can make a choice. Keeping important information in the shadows or masking its message in allegories is of no benefit. I think it should be made easy and accessible to everyone, even to those for whom it may be premature, who might not be ready for it. I passionately believe that it's important that people have access to as much information as possible so they can make up their own mind. They are free to accept or reject whatever it is that they are exposed to. Assisting our fellow man in their Spiritual evolution has value, as long as it is requested. Unsolicited preaching of views or beliefs is never a good thing. Help must be wanted and requested, which is implied when one reads a book. A book is an offer of help, but nothing more.

Anyway, after first reading Dr. Hawkins' second book in his series about Spirituality called *The Eye of the I – From Which Nothing Is Hidden*, (I chose to read this before his first book in that series, titled *Power Vs Force*), I felt compelled to meet this man.

I was lucky.

At the time I attempted to contact him, he was still responding to people privately, and he granted me that privilege. When I say "granted," I am 100 percent certain that before agreeing to meet, he had fully vetted me, using his methods to understand my intentions as well as my calibrated level of consciousness. Only after passing this pre-qualification did his office contact me to let me know that the meeting would take place.

We met in his office at his home in Sedona, Arizona. I had no idea what to expect and, honestly, the experience surprised me. We didn't talk as much as I had expected and hoped, which was mildly disappointing because I came armed with so many questions. He quickly disarmed me of those, stating that the point of this meeting was to just "share the energy." This was not to be an intellectual exercise, though we did have much conversation. It was experiential. Before long, I rapidly sensed the energy of which he spoke. First, I felt a comfortable vibration moving through my body. Then, I was confronted by a peculiar sensation that was simultaneously unsettling yet also very pleasant. The energy became so strong that I felt like I was floating several inches above my chair.

This floating sensation dissipated as soon as our time was up. The entire session had been a full thirty minutes, but it seemed to start and end with the snap of a finger. Though disappointed that we never addressed most of my questions, I left thinking the meeting was great, unbelievable, and had been exactly what it was supposed to be.

Two days later I attended one of his weekend seminar events — an all-day affair — during which he lectured for about four or five hours, with a lunch break sandwiched in between. The information and energy he shared that day with all five hundred attendees was intense and penetrating. When it was over, and after my forty-five-minute drive back to Flagstaff, Arizona, where I was staying with a friend, I felt the vibrations run through my body again. This time the sensations of energy coursing through my body were so highly charged, intense, and profound that I was literally forced to sit on the floor against a wall in a quiet area in a large hall where my friend was making final adjustments for a banquet she'd arranged for over one hundred people. I needed to ground myself.

After about twenty minutes, I was able to stand up and rejoin my friends, but those vibrations lasted many hours longer and they couldn't have been any more pleasant. Every inch of me didn't want them to end. In fact, at about one in the morning, while comfortably seated in my friend's small, mountain home, as we discussed the Dr. Hawkins seminar I'd attended earlier, the energy that had been coursing through my body for seven hours actually transferred from me, to her. She also was a fan of the doctor's work and I was pleasantly surprised when she declared that her body had begun vibrating, too.

I am certain the meeting I had with Dr. Hawkins and the seminar were experiences I was destined to have. They were answers to my requests for greater understanding and Spiritual direction and awakened a new level of awareness within me. They also recharged my curiosity and spawned a desire within me to change my approach. I realized I had to look inward for my answers. With this realization, the doorway to experiential learning had opened for me. I walked straight in.

My studies to that point were more about gaining knowledge. It had been an intellectual pursuit. I'd already had many experiential lessons along the way, but I hadn't come to the realization that experiential learning was the real teacher; that only through experience could one find real wisdom and create the greatest impact on one's growth and personal power. Sure, the intellectual approach did lead to progress, but it was slow. I felt like I wasn't getting closer to my desired destination: a full understanding of who I am, who we are, what the universe is and, ultimately, how to obtain enlightenment.

I finally understood that I'd been missing one critical thing... Experiential learning. Wisdom is not learned from books. It is experiential and it comes from within.

There's an expression often used that comes across as vague: "from the heart." I'm sure that you have probably heard this or something like it, but have you stopped to think about what it *really* means? To start, it's not a meaningless or esoteric metaphor or platitude. It means exactly what it says.

The heart is not just a muscle pumping blood through the body. There is an energy center within the body located in the middle of the chest, the same area as the heart muscle. This energy center is the Spiritual "heart" and is directly connected to the God Self I mentioned in the previous chapter. This heart has many functions. Perhaps the most important one is that the God Self uses the heart center to communicate with and guide us. For us to benefit from it, though, to take full advantage of its sage advice, we must listen. We must be consciously aware of and aligned to this voice within. This is what awareness and higher consciousness is all about.

This is the voice I'd heard in my early years, before my teens. The key to hearing its voice and its wisdom, and to truly incorporate its wisdom into one's everyday perspective and life, is to recognize and experience the energies we already have within us, and to clear away all the *debris and distractions* that separate us from them. This is the true nature of Spirituality.

Spirituality is this, and only this: Becoming aware of the Inner Selves and actively listening to, and discerning between, the different aspects and voices within, and then making choices based on their guidance. There is nothing more to it. How one reaches this goal — becomes that person who recognizes and listens to their Spiritual selves — is a personal choice. There are many roads leading to this destination. It does not matter which road is taken, as long as we arrive at the true destination. But there is a catch. It is easy to delude ourselves by listening to the wrong inner voice and believing it to be the best one.

Therein lies the real challenge — accurately discerning between the different voices within. This is where many get confused and it's not surprising that this is the case. It takes practice to know which voice is which, to know whether it's the voice of Love or the voice of fear. While this may seem an easy call, I assure you it is not. One voice actively tries to control you and your life — for your protection, it would claim — often deceiving you and manipulating your thoughts to keep you in a nice, safe, little box, while pushing you to experiences and choices that might not be in your best interest, all to fill the void that is the emptiness within. The other voice is more expansive, open, and fearless. It is Love. But it's also very quiet, passive and allowing. So, I ask: To which voice are you listening? The answer to this question is the task at hand.

3

Misadventures of Identity

One thing leads almost everyone astray. I call it *misidentification*. To define this, think about a police lineup with several potential perpetrators. It's your job to identify the right person, the one who committed the crime. You make a choice and feel good, proud of your contribution.

In a Spiritual context, misidentification is similar, but it's not about identifying someone or something outside of yourself. It is about how we identify with ourselves. Do you identify with a political party and political party preferences? Or do you identify as your job or religious affiliation — I'm a doctor, a businessperson, a housekeeper? What about your marital status, gender identity, or as a mother or father?

Misidentification is not about any of those in particular. But it's also about all of them. In my world, misidentification is about how you see and present yourself. It's about how you identify, define yourself, and the limitations a false sense of self can impose. Do you see and identify yourself as a teacher, lawyer, farmer, construction worker, man, woman, heterosexual, homosexual, doctor, businessperson, athlete, husband, wife, mother, or father?

Maybe you'd say you're more than one of these. Maybe none of them. But ask yourself how you identity. How do you think about yourself? How do you present yourself to others?

Almost everyone has had a conversation with someone that went something like this:

Person one: "Tell me something about yourself."
Person two: "Well... I am a writer and Spiritual teacher."

Seems normal enough, right? But there's a potential problem with the words "I am" in the sentence "I am a writer and Spiritual teacher." Even though this statement has an element of truth, when the words "I am" are used in this way they sometimes contain a hidden agenda: the job of creating "status" or self-importance and often are accompanied by an inflated sense of self. There's also an unstated implication that whatever label one has latched onto — and then projects outwardly to the world — is who they *are*. If you label yourself in this way, you are doing your Spiritually complex self a disservice by devaluing your essence and true potential in this world and beyond. Sure, you may have participated in or experienced one or more of these sorts of things, and that's great. But that's not who you *are*.

Take a moment and think about the questions I'm about to ask and be brutally honest with yourself. How do you introduce yourself to others? How do you describe yourself to new acquaintances? When speaking to someone you just met, do you immediately attempt to associate yourself with your job or with some type of activity or life situation, especially one in which you excel and take pride? Do you feel that presenting yourself in this way brings some level of importance and respect in the world?

If so, you're not alone, and don't let this realization upset you. Most people do this. We confuse our true nature — who we really are — with our tastes, preferences, accomplishments, jobs, and other outer world experiences. It's a search for validation from sources outside of ourselves often intended to fill an inner feeling of emptiness.

Certainly, the descriptive comment, "I am a writer" may simply be innocently spoken words that are intended to provide some information during a conversation — that I spend some of my time writing. For many, though, reliance on these types of self-created labels could also be a symptom of a deeper issue, like being shy or guarded around people, as one example. A shy person might feel the inner need to justify their reason for being somewhere, like a party. This is where identity gets messy. They conflate their true nature with their life experiences in an attempt to feel comfortable, validated.

The labels we assign to ourselves are not who we are. They may be things we do; ways to make a living or experiences we enjoy. Mostly, though, they're just activities that occupy some of our time as we go through our lives. The mistake people often make — and most do, to some degree — is latching onto these things in an unnatural and unhealthy way. This can lead to disappointment and a deepening unhappiness when these things aren't going well, or as planned, which is almost inevitable at some point in life.

We find comfort in our labels. We use them to foster a narrative for ourselves, a façade, which we present to others to explain who we think we are. By identifying with our labels, we create a narrow definition of ourselves. We allow them to usurp our real identity and use them as masks to hide who we truly are, even from ourselves. At the end of the day, they are just illusions but we give them power. We use them to feel more important, validated, which helps us feel better about who we are in our competitive world, even if only temporarily. But this also has a downside. When these illusions change or fail us, the false comfort they've created can collapse, leaving us in a state of despair and disappointment.

On a basic level, is it really so bad to use these labels to define ourselves? Probably not. However, our use of labels cannot be viewed in a vacuum with the assumption that nothing else in our lives is affected by them. As with most things, there's a bigger picture to consider.

When we place too much importance on things like these labels, we also reinforce the grand misconception we have about ourselves as human beings. This sort of identity association encourages us to lose sight of who we really are, and supports the fantasy created and projected by the Ego self. The more we define ourselves with our labels based on our past achievements and future desires, the more we become separated from our True Self, the real source of our power. The True Self holds the key to create real success, authentic inner peace and contentment, lasting happiness, and Love.

If moving closer to the higher reality of our true nature is the goal, we must overcome these sorts of delusional thinking patterns. Our delusions hinder our freedom to experience and express ourselves in the world, as well as our real potential to create and contribute beauty and Love. Limitation is never a good thing. Expansion is a fundamental component of consciousness and ultimately each one of us is a pure expression of consciousness, so the path of continual expansion is the most direct way to become our best selves.

Here's a truth I'd like to share: You are far greater than the things you do for a living, or your hobbies, or the activities you enjoy. In fact, you are God in every sense of that word. This fact has been long forgotten, creating a void within. Erroneously, we attempt to fill that void with misidentifications: the labels we give ourselves.

So, how does the negative power of misidentification take hold? What is its source?

These questions speak directly to the principles and very foundation of Spirituality. Spirituality is the discovery, awareness, and study of the Inner Selves. With practice, you will discover that the misidentification problem and, in turn, nearly all our other problems, originate from the same source: the Ego self. As mentioned in chapter 3, *Unmasking Reality*, the Ego self is one of the two aspects of the Individualized Self. We all have an Ego self and it will dominate the Individualized Self if we allow it.

Here's why knowing this is essential. The Ego self is based in fear. That, by itself, is not a bad thing. The fear contained in the Ego self can serve a noble purpose: to create balance with the True Self, which can be naïve about the physical world, protecting us from actual danger; real physical harm. For example, the Ego self and its healthy, rational fear draws important and helpful boundaries around our lives, such as stopping us from jumping off a tall building. The Ego self also provides more depth and feeling to the experience of being human in the three-dimensional, physical world. The Ego self feels things more deeply, which helps us enjoy this world to a greater degree.

Alerting us to actual physical danger is the function of healthy fear offered by the Ego self. Healthy fear helps keep us physically safe and therefore alive. However, the Ego self goes astray when it's not kept in check. It wants to control our lives and will go to extremes to do so. To accomplish this, the Ego self creates a long list of *unhealthy* fears, such as the fear of rejection, the fear of failure, the fear that we are not enough just as we are, and many others. It creates a false equivalency, associating these illusory fears with actual danger and physical harm, and ultimately uses them to keep us stagnant, often stopping us from taking measured risks that can lead to personal growth and expansion of consciousness.

Unhealthy fears do two things, neither of them positive. They have a misguided protective component, erroneously stopping us from doing things that *may* end in failure and create emotional distress. This limits our opportunities for new experiences and our likelihood for greater success. Unhealthy fears also bring unpleasant feelings, which are used by the Ego self to fill the inner emptiness many of us experience. This emptiness will always be filled with whatever is available in the moment. So, if unhealthy fear is generated, it will be used to fill the void that should be filled with Love. It is never positive when fear takes a place that could be filled with Love.

Regardless of the term used to describe these unpleasant feelings, they can encourage us to look outside of ourselves to feel better, which seems like a noble cause. We just want to feel good about our lives, our place in the world, and ourselves. To accomplish this, though, we invent illusions and latch onto them. One such illusion is a false identity. Latching onto the self-identifiers listed earlier in this chapter is a strong Ego self strategy to limit us and control our lives. These are powerful lures — we squeeze our labels tightly to hide and feel protected from the world.

The misidentifications, or labels, we take on are the domain and power of the Ego self. Learning to recognize these occurrences and the energies behind them is a vital step in advancing your awareness — consciousness — and will increase your level of comfort with yourself and the world and your overall level of happiness.

4

The Ego self

The Ego self is an exasperating aspect of our humanness. When I discuss the Ego self, I'm not referring to the behaviors some people exhibit that cause others to label them egomaniacs. Grandiose gestures done strictly to draw attention to oneself are readily seen in our society. It appears that these have become more common and accepted in recent years as our society drowns itself in a sea of social media "likes" and "comments." Selfies — when individuals take and post pictures of themselves on social media — are a prime example of this. Taking a picture of oneself isn't a problem in itself, but when it is done to excess for no reason other than to receive the validation and admiration of others online, that is indicative of a problem.

Make no mistake, these sorts of behaviors do emanate from the aforementioned Ego self. But these are examples of the *outward* manifestations it creates. When I discuss the Ego self, I am referencing a specific part of the *inner* makeup and essence of all humans.

We all have an Ego self. Each individual has their own particular version of it. Based on experiences and other factors, your Ego self has taken on different affectations than mine. But they both originate from the same source. What's interesting, and what many might not know or even believe, is that the Ego self is created by the God Self. It is a temporary aspect of ourselves and, unlike the True Self and the Individualized Self, it only comes alive at birth. It ceases when the body dies — when its primary fear is realized — but it doesn't completely disappear. Some of its proclivities and affectations are imprinted upon the Individualized Self and, if needed, will be addressed in future incarnations and life experiences.

Based on what I've already written about the Ego Self, you might presume that I believe it is, by nature, a negative component of our humanity. Certainly, it can be interpreted that way. And, when left unchecked, it can and will have a devastating impact on ourselves and our world. It is the source of all hatred, anger, disappointment, and many other things and experiences people usually wish to eliminate from their lives and the world.

The Ego self has created major frustrations, failures, and emotional pain in my life. I'm sure it has in yours, too. As negative as the things created by the Ego self can be and, certainly, they can be awful, the Ego self is not a negative aspect of ourselves. Ultimately, it just *is*. It is a valuable component of our reality that we must accept and Love, just as we'd Love an innocent child learning about the world. On the other hand, it is up to each one of us to choose to develop self-awareness so that we can keep it in check, even teach it, and to limit its influence and reduce the potential damage and disasters it can create. The goal is to choose to allow Love to be in control. Love is the foundation and domain of the True Self.

The Ego self and the True Self — which together form the Individualized Self — are both created by the God Self. They are not, themselves, the God Self. They are individual offshoots, but also connected to it, like separate branches of the same tree. And, just as branches serve the tree, sprouting leaves which photosynthesize carbon dioxide and light to create food so it can grow and thrive, the Individualized Self and its two components serve the God Self within, providing experiences which allow the God Self and, thus, the Greater God (consciousness), to grow. The Individualized Self is the aspect of ourselves most of us believe to be who we are. But we are much more than that.

The Individualized Self is in a constant state of conflict. Its components, the True Self and the Ego self, do not usually agree. In fact, they're usually going in very different directions, each having their own desires and ideas about what course life should take, from the more ordinary decisions like what to eat for breakfast, to the more significant choices like who to select as a life partner. There's a major difference between these two aspects of you, and this difference is the most important thing to know about them, and yourself: The Ego self is completely and utterly motivated by fear, whereas the True Self is completely and utterly motivated by Love. This is why they are often in opposition and is why the decision-making process can be messy. Since the decisions we make — the choices we make for ourselves and for others who depend on us — shape our experiences, successes, failures, and loves, the Ego self/True Self duality within is a major factor in determining the direction your life will take.

Things can be easy for us, or they can be hard. We can make good decisions and we can make bad ones. We can have a life that is filled with more joy, or a life of constant struggle, disappointment, and sadness. All this is up to us. Our experiences and results are simply outcomes of the decisions we make. So, it only makes sense to become aware of your inner motivations, to understand the cogs that turn beneath the surface and how these actively shape and determine your choices.

Although the Ego self is fear based, it is an offspring of the God Self. This is important to understand because it demonstrates that the Ego self is not inherently bad. And, like the True Self, it is given freedom. The freedom afforded to the Ego self is identical to that given to the True Self; the gift of free will, which is bestowed at the time of their creation.

For humans, free will and choice begins at birth and is given to the Individualized Self and its two components by the God Self within. This gift, though, does come with challenges and responsibilities. One responsibility we all have is to make choices that are in harmony with oneself, as well as with one's neighbors, community, the planet, and universe.

Problems arise when these responsibilities are ignored. And, unfortunately, most do ignore this responsibility, though this ignorance usually is not malicious in nature. Some people, however, do have malicious intent. Extreme examples are the great despots and murderous leaders and dictators who, throughout history, rose to power to dominate, enslave, and exterminate others. Most people, though, make poor choices due to a lack of information about themselves and our world, and sometimes a more innocent yet selfish failure to consider the consequences of their actions.

There are other, perhaps deeper reasons for poor choices. One certainly is that our free will and choice does offer those predisposed to walk a darker path — to create pain and suffering for others — an open invitation to do so. This is one of the complications of being free to do and experience whatever we desire and, as you might imagine, is the result of an Ego self in complete control of the Individualized Self. Love would never make these sorts of choices. Only fear treads in these waters. This freedom is made even more "free" due to this additional, crucial piece of our collective reality: we are not judged for our choices. The God Self does not judge. If the God Self did judge, and then administered consequences for our poor choices, would the gift of free will and choice really be just that, free will and choice? Or would it be less than free; subject to factors that would ultimately shape our actions just to please the God Self?

We would not be free if we were judged in that way, as potential consequences for some choices would create a price to be paid, meaning that our choices were not entirely our own. That's more akin to coercion, than it is to freedom. So, in the Spiritual realms, there is no judgment for the choices we make, regardless of how harmful they may be.

On the physical plane, however, there is judgment. Laws have been put into place by humans — often abiding by Spiritual or religious principles (sometimes rightly, sometimes wrongly) — which are necessary to protect ourselves from one another. The consequences of breaking these laws can be substantial, and appropriately so. Spiritually speaking, though, it is up to each one of us to choose to be good. But being a good, responsible, fair-minded, and considerate person is merely an option (a good one at that). It is not a requirement. It is up to each one of us to choose who and what we desire to be and which paths we will travel to get there.

Although judgement does not exist in the Spiritual realms, justice does. It exists through the universal Law of Karma. Karma is a concept in both the Hindu and Buddhist religions that speaks to cause and effect. Briefly, it states that you are the sum-total of your actions, and what you do today could significantly impact your future, and future lives. Your actions have consequences. As I see it, Karma is not intended to be a punishment, though. Karma provides us with the opportunity to experience and learn so that we can grow and expand as individual components of consciousness and our universe, or what I refer to as "the Greater God." So, choosing wisely is preferable, and the rewards of these choices are enormous in both the physical and Spiritual worlds.

Given that there is no judgment, in the absence of inner awareness, the Ego self can operate with the freedom of a fox in a hen house. Since the Ego self operates from fear, and often without regard for others, it is perfectly logical that almost all the poor choices we make can be traced back to the Ego self.

A major contributor to this situation comes down to this: The Ego self has an overpowering voice. It demands attention, acknowledgement, and capitulation. Think of a child having a tantrum in the middle of a restaurant, loudly screaming. That's what the Ego self does inside of us to influence our decisions and external behaviors. And we let it. We've given it our power. Over time, in fact, we become so comfortable with it and its antics that we don't realize this is happening. This is the subtle way the Ego self controls us — influencing what we think, say, and do. It is demanding, unyielding, uncompromising, and cunning. It will do everything possible to control the choices we make and to get its way. Exacerbating this problem is that the Ego self usually has its own agenda, which might not be the best for us, and can be damaging to others around us.

Everything we do and create is through choices made by the Individualized Self. To review what we've discovered so far, the Individualized Self is comprised of both the Ego self and the True Self and these two have their own list of desires, wants, and needs.

These are presented to the Individualized Self — the aspect of you that you would describe as *me* — and it (you) makes choices based on the inputs it receives from the Ego self and the True Self. This is how these two aspects collectively decide the path we take in life. But, as mentioned earlier, these two are often at odds and usually have very different desires, goals, and motivations.

As the Ego self is motivated by fear and the True Self is motivated by Love, it can seem like they are on opposite ends of the spectrum. This is often true, but not always. Regardless, this duality within can complicate the decision-making process, even if we're completely unaware of this internal battle raging inside. It's a conflict of attention and dominance — Love versus fear. Those less aware may experience no confusion at all, as the Ego self is so dominant that they have no idea that a True Self also exists within and has something to offer. But a lack of confusion doesn't mean they're making the best choices. It only means that these folks are *unconsciously* moving through life. It is only through deliberate and focused development of inner awareness that this duality becomes apparent. This is the beginning of our *awakening*, which offers the benefit of making conscious decisions and choices that will lead to better outcomes, including a more successful, fulfilling, and joyful life.

In the earliest stages of developing this awareness, look to the physical body and any sensations you may feel within the body. This is the quickest path to developing higher consciousness and is the easiest method to immediately implement. It only requires a minor change in focus from what you see and sense in the outer world, to what's going on within, to the world of your Inner Selves. Pay closer attention to the messages your body sends you. What do you feel? Do you feel angst in your gut? Or do you sense a more comfortable feeling in your heart? Remember that your body is a communication tool. It will inform you if something is right or wrong and will tell you about the battles raging inside.

As loud the voice of the Ego self is, the opposite is true for the True Self, making awareness of our inner battles even more difficult. The True Self's voice is incredibly quiet. Its desires and motivations always come from pure Love and Love is both powerful, yet also subtle; it is not loud and forceful. Love allows. It never imposes its will. The True Self will never force itself on the Ego self and, thus, on us.

So, to hear the voice of the True Self, one must actively pursue it. One must choose it. And the choice to hear, identify with, and react from the True Self must be made over and over, day after day. In the overall puzzle of life, these are moment-to-moment choices. To live and make our choices purely from the perspective of the True Self, we must develop moment-to-moment awareness.

This is the foundation, the first stage, from which Enlightenment ultimately springs. Enlightenment is nothing more than the internal awareness of the different aspects within, and the active and conscious choice to identify with, listen to, and react from the True Self. Once this has been mastered, then additional pathways and dimensions of Enlightenment will be revealed.

When connected to and resonating with the True Self, one is said to be in a "state of grace." When one does otherwise, defaulting back to the Ego self, that is a "fall from grace."

Unfortunately, that "fallen" state of being — when we choose to identify with the Ego self and react to others and our world from its perspective and make choices based on its intentions and desires — has become the default or even the preferred way of life for most. We weren't born this way and most don't consciously choose this. As we grow up, though, most of us are snared by this trap. This fall from grace, creating an illusionary identity based on the Ego self, has become our chosen state of being. If there is a *devil*, and there is not, it would be the Ego self. It, alone, is the source of all evil in our world.

The Ego self takes charge and that's the way the Ego self wants it. The result for many is a silent battle within that can be a killer of dreams and an obstacle to true contentment and happiness. This also is the reason that the world is in such bad shape, and getting worse. We worship the Ego self, and having lost our awareness of the True Self, poor choices have become the norm, reaching pandemic-like levels and causing much of the misery, disappointment, and negativity in our lives and the world at large.

When terrible things happen people often wonder, "How can God do this to us?" The answer should now be coming into focus. God is Love. Love is allowing. God does not judge. It is not God which creates the problems we see. The Ego self is the one doing this creating. God simply stands back, allows, and watches with Love.

Awareness is the solution. It enables the process to heal ourselves, to transcend the fear-based influence of the Ego self, and reconnect with the True Self and its genuine Love.

5

The True Self

L et's take a deeper dive into the True Self. For most people, the True Self has become more of a silent counterbalance to the Ego self, but it was not meant to be that way. The True Self should be the dominant aspect in our lives.

At the time of our birth, the God Self creates the Ego self and places it with the True Self. To illustrate how these two come to be, and their relationship to one another and to the God Self, picture an ovary within a woman's body releasing a pair of eggs. These eggs, though separate and distinct from the mother, are part of the mother, each carrying its own unique version of the mother's DNA.

In the same manner, the True Self and the Ego self are not only created by the God Self, they also are equal parts of the God Self. These two are bound together to form the Individualized Self, which (as discussed earlier) is how most of us identify ourselves.

The Individualized Self is who we think we are, our identity, and for most of us — likely over 99.9 percent of us — it is dominated by the Ego self to some degree. This will vary by individual according to their level of consciousness.

The job each of us share is to become aware of our Inner Selves and to use this awareness to learn and grow from life's experiences. It is our task to understand how all the energies inside us behave and work to influence our decisions, actions, and our lives. Having this awareness puts us in a position to make better choices — conscious choices — and to create a better life for ourselves, as well as a better world. In the absence of this awareness, life can unfold randomly and chaotically. As we go through life, we have to continually make a choice. We must choose which aspect of Inner Selves we'd like to resonate with — live, act, and react from. We are free to choose the guidance and perspective offered by the True Self and its energy and essence of Love, or the Ego Self and its darker, fear-based perspectives. A proper and appropriate blending of the two, where Love is in charge and fear is subservient, is the goal. This choice is always there, even for those who have reached the highest levels of enlightenment. However, for them, it is likely an easier decision to make.

Therefore, our main true purpose in life is to learn to consciously choose the True Self and its Love. With some exceptions, anything else you may accomplish or experience in this life is not really your purpose. Instead, it may be useful to view these as things of interest, or activities you like to do, even if the True Self is the source of the desire to do them.

In fact, you can and will be guided by the True Self, even if you don't hear its quiet advice. It will find a way to encourage you to act and accomplish specific things. For almost everyone, its guidance will be experienced through subtle signals within the body, like a vibration or a gut instinct, and each signal will point you in a relevant direction. It is, therefore, critical to continually monitor the reactions within your body. Let it communicate to you, rather than you imposing your feelings on it.

Those who have developed a higher degree of inner awareness might also be guided in other ways. These can include hearing an inner voice or seeing answers in the mind's eye. If this happens to you, do your best to pay attention to this guidance and act accordingly. People that do this tend to be the happier among us. Unfortunately, in today's world, most ignore this guidance. The reason for this is relatively easy to define but a little more complicated to remedy: many of us have disconnected from our Inner Selves. We lack this inner awareness. This disconnection likely occurred at some time between childhood and young adulthood when, for many people, the True Self can be overwhelmed, even silenced by the demands of the Ego self.

This transformation is neither good nor bad. In the absence of proper Spiritual guidance and training, it's just the typical pattern most experience as they go through life. They learn, grow, and adapt to the experiences and circumstances to which they are exposed. But in the absence of internal awareness, their lives can become unnatural and more difficult. This can be remedied by successfully completing the formidable task of reconnecting with their Inner Selves and relearning how to discern between the competing voices within. If we don't embark upon this life-altering journey, there's a high probability that we'll go through life oblivious to the fact that greater happiness, Love, and fulfillment are calling, even if we believe we already are happy. Many fail to answer this call.

Our task is made even more difficult by the different essences and energies that are the Ego self and the True Self, which results in a perfect environment for an inner battle between fear (Ego self) and Love (True Self). These competing forces both vie for your attention, but the True Self takes a more relaxed, allowing, and almost silent approach.

Fear can be overwhelming. It can cause highly distracting mental and physiological reactions that demand to be heard and recognized immediately. It acts and reacts this way because it perceives everything from a perspective of life and death. As a result, fear can be paralyzing as it shouts for our attention and clouds our thinking — often deluding us into making poor choices, wrongly choosing what we think will be best for us, but is not. Although something like a panic attack is an extreme example of this, fear can be, and usually is, much more subtle. It quietly operates in the background, hidden beyond our immediate awareness. The Ego self uses this subtle approach to exert its control and to maintain the illusion that everything is "normal" and "fine," while concealing the fact that it is influencing our choices. In this way, it maintains its control without us even realizing that this is happening. The Ego self can be tricky in that way — cunning — using all sorts of subtle tactics to keep its power. The solution to this problem is internal awareness and paying attention to how you feel.

Love, on the other hand, works in the opposite way. Think of a good mother allowing her child to make a mistake so her child can learn from that mistake. (Good parenting demands this. Parents who step in to protect their children are not doing them any favors unless, of course, their lives or limbs are immediately at risk.) A good parent regards their child with pure Love and allows the child to stumble, and then reviews the situation with them in a patient and loving way to help them learn from their mistakes. That's Love.

Love is allowing, but not loud. Love waits patiently to be acknowledged; it does not demand. Love sits back hoping that it is freely *chosen* by the object of its affection. Forced acknowledgment, or feelings brought about by expectation, is not valid Love. Real Love knows this. So, it stays in the background until it is actively sought. Then, once it is sought, it will respond by offering — not imposing or demanding — all its gifts. The True Self already exists within you, quietly waiting for you to seek and discover it. It is up to you to build a bridge to reconnect with its essence and energy.

The True Self does, however, offer its guidance to us even when we're not connected and are not actively listening. It never leaves us alone. It just does its job in very subtle ways through deep feelings. It never ignores us. It is we who ignore it. One of the main reasons many feel alone in life is because they choose to overlook the voice of the True Self. It is up to each of us to acknowledge and speak directly to it. When you decide to open the lines of communication, it will answer. We just need to develop the awareness and concentration to hear its "voice" in whatever form that takes. For many, the lack of connection to this part of themselves is the emptiness felt within; the feeling that they are not satisfied with life no matter how much money, success, and Love they may have. The endless pursuit of those things to fill the inner emptiness is a misguided effort. Simply look within and find your True Self and the hole will begin to fill.

There are times, though, when ideas that form the foundation for success do come from the True Self, even if one is disconnected from it and has no awareness that it is the source. If you are destined for something, and have chosen a specific experience for this life, the True Self will find a way to get that information to you when the time is right. Dreams are one way it might communicate. Dreams strip away the Ego self and its distractions and can carry messages directly from the True Self.

Have you ever awakened with a strong feeling about a problem or decision you have been considering; with a new feeling one way or the other that was not there before you fell asleep? Depending on what that feeling was, and what actions it may have compelled you to take, it could have been the True Self guiding you, quietly communicating its ideas. And this advice could have been offered even if you are consciously disconnected from this powerful part of yourself, as most are.

I experienced this exact scenario. In 1986, I was still living in my small apartment in the East Village in New York City. During a visit with my family in Florida, my father introduced me to an interesting concept for an advertising related business. He knew I was looking for a business to start and believed this was a great idea for several reasons. I agreed. I liked the idea. It was easy to get into and was aligned with the business skills I'd had. Given all that, though, after a few hours of consideration, something didn't feel right and I went to sleep that night believing it was not the right business for me. I'd decided not to pursue it. However, I awoke the next morning with a complete change in perspective. The shift was dramatic. I was all in. Without another thought, I had decided to uproot my entire life — quite my job, move to Florida and start that very business, which I ultimately did. I did not know this then, but now know that this change was the result of my True Self guiding me. For many reasons, it was time for me to live in Florida, which was not my desire at all, but was where I'd planned to be for a large segment of this life, (planned before my birth to this life), and this business was a vehicle to take me there.

Conflicts arise when the Ego self gets involved. This is inevitable. It does not matter whether you'd like input from the Ego self or not. It will make its demands and insert itself and its desires whenever it feels the slightest bit threatened. This is true even for those who've done the job of developing a conscious relationship with their Inner Selves and the True Self, and have learned to discern between the two voices within. The Ego self will always try to assert itself. Therefore, without vigilance, the possibility always exists that one could abandon the guidance offered by the True Self simply because it is overpowered by the voice of the Ego self. Continual monitoring of the Inner Selves is paramount, even for the most highly aware and conscious among us.

The True Self does want to be heard. To activate this powerful part of your inner makeup, it is useful to remind yourself that it will not impose or force itself upon you. You must ask it for its advice. This, unfortunately, is very easy to forget or overlook.

Each of us has the freedom to make our own choices, whatever they may be. We always have the option available to move forward unconsciously, making our choices based on the Ego self and its fear-based perspective. Or we can choose more consciously from the perspective of the True Self and its Love. It is possible that the choice we make will be the same regardless of which perspective guides us, but the best option is to ask the True Self for its help in attaining or experiencing whatever it is that you truly desire, and then listen for the answer. This will put the odds of success and happiness in your favor. These are the hidden battles within, the inner conflicts we all must overcome. The arena where this plays out is the realm of the Individualized Self, which I'll discuss in the next couple of chapters.

6

The Individualized Self

N ow we come to what I call the Individualized Self —
the part of you that you would traditionally identify as,
well, you. This is who you *think* you are. It also is the
part of you who asks questions, seeks answers, and is responsible
for your happiness and unhappiness with life. The Individualized
Self is the aspect of you that has self-awareness. It is the component that can be blinded by the demanding voice of the Ego self,
to the detriment of the True Self, and is often unaware of the inner
conflicts between those two.

Feeling angry? That comes from the Individualized Self.
Disappointed? Frustrated? Satisfied? Exhilarated? Same origin.

The Individualized Self is the aspect of you that forms your tastes, preferences, desires, and joys.

While it is okay to identify with the Individualized Self to some extent, it is useful to note that most of the problems in our lives, and in the world, do come from it. This, as already discussed, is true when the dominant aspect of the Individualized Self is the Ego self. For most of us — probably about 99 percent of the world's population, maybe more — the Ego self is in control and that's the way the Ego self wants it to be. The wise among us make it a priority to be aware of its urgent demands and to temper or counter them when appropriate. Once we become consciously aware of the Ego self's cunning nature, the Individualized Self is then able to employ a more balanced approach to the decision-making process. We can assert our power over the Ego self, giving ourselves the opportunity to make better choices. It is up to each of us to either accept the forceful directives injected by the Ego self or reject them and choose differently. We always have the option to hear and accept the subtle guidance offered by the True Self. It is the Individualized Self who has this option.

Side note: The emphasis many place on their "identity" can be unhealthy. It feeds the Ego self and its fears, enabling it and its power to expand. The way we present ourselves to others is often a façade designed to impress and to hide our perceived faults from them. It is a protective mechanism engineered by the Ego self, but doing this consumes our creative energies that, if applied differently — more appropriately — might yield better results in our lives. In fact, a large portion of our valuable creative energy is wasted constructing and maintaining these illusions. Wouldn't it be easier to simply be who we really are, and to then use all that squandered energy to create the life, Love, and successes we really desire?

Remember, the Ego self operates from a place of fear. However, unless real physical danger is immediately involved, fear is never the right energy, intent, or motivation for assessing life, making decisions, or reacting to the people and situations life throws your way. But most people have unknowingly aligned themselves with the Ego self, and they do rely on the energy of its unnatural and unhealthy fears as the basis for everything they do. This does impact their decisions, actions, and reactions. Those taken from this perspective tend to be more emotional and since these particular emotions are based in the very subtle energy of unhealthy fear — the foundation of the Ego self — the likelihood of unwanted situations and outcomes usually increases.

Giving the Ego self free reign over your life is a haphazard way to live. More times than not, this is likely to yield negative results. So, how to place the odds more in your favor? This is where awareness of the Inner Selves becomes essential. You, as the Individualized Self, have the power to choose to hear and consider input from the True Self. Both are there for your benefit. Ultimately, the Ego self and the True Self are equal partners within the Individualized Self. They both have the capacity through their influence to shape and control our lives. They both have the ability to create things for you, and for the world. So, what's the main takeaway from this? The Ego self always creates from fear, which can lead to disastrous results. The True Self creates from Love.

You can shape and create your life from either fear or Love — so which are you choosing? Love is always better than fear. Better for ourselves and better for the world. Everything we do, for ourselves and for others, carries a greater impact than most realize. The energies behind our actions create energy waves which emanate from the core of ourselves, from our heart-center. These ripple out from us and into universe, similar to the effect created when a rock is thrown into a still, mirror-like pond. In this way, everything we think and do affects our world. Ultimately, these waves return to us like a boomerang. Therefore, acting and creating from the energy and essence of Love is always a better choice than fear.

It is up to each of us to resolve the differences between the True Self and the Ego self. You, the Individualized Self, are the arbiter. The Individualized Self gets to be the mediator between these two selves but, obviously, awareness that they even exist is necessary. Whatever course of action you choose will add to your life's experiences, so choose wisely. Awareness is the key. You now know that the Ego self has the louder voice. It screams and carries on like a baby having a tantrum to gain our attention and impose its will. At the same time, the True Self is content to remain quietly in the background until it is actively called upon. It will not impose itself. We all have this choice to make. It is up to you to consciously choose one or the other, or a blending of the two. Which makes more sense? Which offers the potential for more expansive and fulfilling experiences?

This is where awareness comes into play. When we make our choices *without* the awareness that we are being influenced by these inner aspects of ourselves, we are said to be *unconscious* or *asleep*. This usually means that we go through life blinded by the fears innate to the Ego self, which can lead to one poor decision after another.

What makes this worse is that the majority of people are unaware of these fears; they hide quietly beneath layers of distracting thoughts, opinions, ideas, and lifetimes of suppressed feelings. They operate from the darkest recesses of ourselves, hidden from any awareness. The main problem is that they are also persistently powerful and powerfully persistent. They are puppet masters. They affect the choices we make and how we think and act. Not recognizing this can, and has, led to disastrous results.

Do you see how, when left invisible, this powerful influencer can make life more difficult? When fear is the decider, the probability that our choices are the best ones for us is greatly reduced.

There are those who have gained this inner awareness. They are the awakened, actively resonating with and living in conscious connection to the True Self. They tend to be happier, even if they are considered less successful according to our modern definitions of success (usually financial).

A critical element of the Individualized Self — even for those living at the highest levels of consciousness — is inner awareness. This includes an awareness of both the Ego self and the True Self, and it must be pursued and employed continuously. Any lapse in this awareness will create an opportunity for the Ego self to impose its will. In every decision, no matter how big or small, you will always have to choose between the loving influence, essence, and energy of the True Self, and the potentially damaging, fear-based demands of the Ego self. As you increase in consciousness, it will become easier to recognize and choose between the two. Even then, though, the choice remains, day to day, moment to moment. This is a fundamental aspect of our gift of free will.

Since the Individualized Self is the one doing the choosing — and you are the Individualized Self personified — and within you resides these two often conflicting influencers, one overtly vying for your attention while the other remains quiet until chosen, awareness is crucial. Have you heard the phrase "careful what you wish for, for you certainly might get it"? That means we can, and we usually do, create things in our lives that we'd rather not experience or be part of. I argue, then, that inner awareness is an antidote to bad choices.

We, as the Individualized Self are the master. Learning to discern between our two inner voices is our choice, but also paramount to happiness. This is the essence and nature of Spirituality.

It's the most important job we have, and it is up to each of us to choose. This is life's true purpose and one that we all share. We each need to make a conscious choice to develop awareness of our Inner Selves and then to choose to listen, react, and identify with the True Self, rather than succumbing to the more imposing, fear-based, Ego self.

Ascending to this level of awareness, to these higher realms of "consciousness," is the essence of enlightenment. It may seem like a daunting task to some but, despite being challenging, enlightenment doesn't have to be as difficult to achieve as it may sound. Attaining this level of consciousness is not required during this lifetime, or even your next one, but it is something all of us ultimately aspire to, whether we realize this or not. So, why not make a conscious choice to pursue it?

Whether you choose to advance your awareness and increase your level of consciousness is completely up to you. But remember: the choice to *not* pursue your Spiritual nature is most likely a choice being championed by the Ego self, as it seeks domination over the True Self. Either way, it is still your choice, and always will be.

You may be wondering how, or even if, any of this applies to you and your life right now. I can assure you with 100 percent certainty that it does. Exactly how it might apply can be seen in the many aspects of life in which we find ourselves, especially when we are overwhelmed or obsessed.

I do realize that this concept can appear a little abstract. Nonetheless, it is very real, and these sorts of inner conflicts continue to rage within each of us all day, every day. In the next chapter, we'll take a look at some real-world examples of conflicts the Individualized Self must work through, and how these can influence our choices and our lives.

7

The Individualized
Self in Action

"Man seeks happiness in pleasure, in joy, but these are only shadows of happiness. The real happiness is in the heart of man. But man does not look for it. In order to find happiness, he seeks pleasure." [2]

[2]   Hazrat Inayat Khan, Wahiduddin's Web, The Spiritual Message of Hazrat Inayat Khan, Volume VI — The Alchemy of Happiness The Purpose Of Life (1), https://wahiduddin.net/mv2/VI/VI_3.htm

"In reality very few in this world know what happiness means. Pleasure is the shadow of happiness, for pleasure depends upon things outside ourselves; happiness comes from within ourselves. Happiness belongs to the heart quality; pleasure to the outer world. The distance between pleasure and happiness is as vast as that between earth and heaven." [3]

I n the last chapter, we discovered the Individualized Self — the outer-world representation of you, me, and everyone around us. As discussed, the Individualized Self is how we see and identify ourselves and how we (often) would like the world to perceive us. The Individualized Self is malleable and changeable.

Our desire for the world to see or perceive us in a specific way is a result of the Ego self's yearning for validation. The Ego self causes all our personal pain, suffering, and disappointment, which usually manifests when its desires are not achieved in a timely manner, or at all. It also creates all the oppression and horrors we see in our world. That being said, the Ego self is not inherently bad. It just *is*. In addition to enhancing our physical world experiences it has a protective function. It uses *healthy* fear, (which is different from *unhealthy* fear — fear of things that don't create physical harm, like disappointments), to keep us safe from real (versus imagined) physical harm.

When asked what they want in life almost every human will say (or at least think) "happiness." Unfortunately, for most, happiness is an endless pursuit. Even worse, the quest for happiness often has the opposite effect, resulting in greater despair. And

[3]   Hazrat Inayat Khan, Wahiduddin's Web, The Spiritual Message of Hazrat Inayat Khan, Volume VIIIa — Sufi Teachings The Tuning Of The Heart (1) https://wahiduddin.net/mv2/VIIIa/VIIIa_4_4.htm

there's a related factor that compounds this problem and it's a sneaky one. This never-ending search for a feeling — one which many people confuse with happiness — can occupy so much of our creative energies that it diminishes our capacity to actively create the life we want. Therefore, the search for this "false" happiness becomes a distraction.

Here's the dilemma: Most people are so detached from their True Self, and its innately joyful view of life, that they don't know what they really want, so happiness becomes abstract — more of an idea to be pursued than a reality to be experienced. And, any happiness one does manage to experience, real or imagined, is fleeting. One moment you feel great, the next, you're wondering why you no longer do, which causes you to resume the search. This can become an endless cycle that, sadly, makes true happiness an unrealized dream for many.

Even though we all want happiness, most of us look to the Ego self to satisfy this powerful urge. Doing so is like trying to catch a fish by casting a line upward from the ground and into the branches of a landlocked tree. Obviously, fish don't live in trees, so such an act is not likely to produce results. Similarly, you're not likely to find real and lasting happiness in the empty well of the Ego self. It just isn't found there. Over time, though, we become too familiar and comfortable with the Ego self and learn to confuse the joy and pleasure it *fabricates* with actual happiness. We make it our default supplier. The unfortunate irony should now be obvious: happiness is something the Ego self cannot supply. The reason for this is simple: The Ego self is too needy. It is the source of an endless craving for validation, admiration, and acceptance and is the origin of the inner emptiness many feel. The Ego self is seeking happiness, too! Therefore, supplying happiness is a job it cannot do. It is not equipped for this task. Happiness is, however, innate — within — waiting to be uncovered and experienced.

The Ego self can be the source of good feelings, such as joy, and it does experience the pleasure and gratification accompanying the physical aspects of emotions like Love. But those things are not happiness. They may feel great but they're merely placebos. However, the Ego self does amplify those types of feelings, which is one reason we become confused and turn to the Ego self for happiness. These feelings are real, but their temporary nature proves they are merely illusions of happiness and not the real deal.

Looking to the Ego self as a source of happiness is a habit that first develops during our adolescent years, when the Ego self takes a more active role and moves to take control of the Individualized Self, pushing the True Self and its softer, more gentle voice to the background. It is useful to remember that we can deconstruct and change habits, which may be desired after awareness of the reliance on the Ego self for happiness comes to light.

Please forgive me. I'm about to repeat myself because I want to impress upon you the importance of the following statement. Happiness that comes from the Ego self is an illusion. And, like all illusions — which ultimately fade away — the illusion of happiness created by the Ego self will evaporate. This evaporation usually happens mere moments after the feeling was first created, but sometimes it takes a little bit longer. Think of the feeling you get when you purchase a new material item. You may feel satisfaction, but that feeling soon fades, and sometimes is followed by indifference, or even disappointment which becomes regret, also known as buyer's remorse. We repeat these types of purchases, as well as other activities, to chase the feeling of happiness that eludes us. It's an endless cycle of unceasing ups and downs, one illusion after another.

The illusions we create to construct happiness are both physical and intellectual. Some of the physical illusions include partying and getting drunk with friends or by oneself; smoking cigarettes;

buying a luxury car, even when it is beyond affordability; having a child; and so on. Almost anything you can think of has the potential to be an idea formed by the Ego self and manifested to create the illusion of happiness.

These activities and experiences are not inherently bad. Upon closer examination, though, most do seem to come with the potential for negative consequences at some level. Intent is the factor that transforms them from simple life experiences to illusions of happiness.

It's always a good idea to examine the intent behind the choices we make. Intent is a major factor in determining whether a particular choice we've made, or an activity in which we participate, is something to create an enjoyable experience — solely for the experience itself — or is an illusionary placebo constructed by the Ego self in its endless search for happiness. There is a difference between genuine enjoyment and a placebo, though this might straddle a very fine line. Is the choice an attempt by the Ego self to fill the inner void, to distract us from the emptiness within? Or is it just an experience not intended to serve any other purpose?

Overcoming the emptiness with placebos is not the real answer. The real answer is to naturally discover the already present internal feelings of completeness, contentment, and satisfaction, even in the absence of any outer world activity, experience, success, or validation. When you do this, you will achieve true happiness. Becoming aware of these particular feelings will properly contextualize all the activities we experience and the choices we make, and since they no longer carry unreasonable expectations, also will increase the satisfaction we get from them.

This is where the True Self comes into play. The way to complete oneself is by increasing awareness of the True Self. The True Self is made of the energy of Love which, when we let it, naturally fills the Individualized Self, including the Ego self, with self-acceptance and true contentment, and will erase any feelings of emptiness. The "void" disappears. The True Self is the path to real happiness, which brings into focus the importance of the continual practice of internal awareness. To connect with the True Self and its peaceful state of being, and *hear* and understand its guidance and answers to your most fundamental questions, it is essential to become aware of the feelings within the body.

Remember, the body is a giant communication tool. To use it, we must employ inner awareness. We've become so preoccupied looking outside of ourselves for answers, validation, and happiness that we've neglected our internal selves. We've learned to rely on our voice, ears, and even our eyes for all communications. But inner awareness is not about these senses. In fact, they, too, can become distractions, leading us away from the answers and truth found in the inner world.

The body uses feelings — physical sensations within the body — to communicate messages from the Ego self, the True Self, and even the God Self. A question to continually ask yourself: What does the physical body feel like internally? Those feelings could be a communication. This leads to the next question to continually ask yourself, which is the most important one: To which internal voice — the True Self or the Ego self — are you listening? That question is the toughest one to accurately answer but is a vital skill to learn and develop. Adding these questions to your daily routine will have enormous benefits. It will increase your capacity for awareness, help you understand yourself and the world, and will lead to better decisions.

Special note: The feeling question noted above is not about thoughts we sometimes label and express as feelings, such as: I am "sad." Many times, these types of emotion-derived *thoughts* are erroneously used to express what we think we *feel*. They are often confused with actual "feelings." Feelings are physical sensations emanating from within the body, especially from the chest (heart) and stomach (solar plexus) areas, but can emanate from anywhere. These can be communications from our Inner Selves offering answers to our questions. An emotional statement about something like sadness, or anything else, when not accompanied by a physical sensation within the body, is not the same thing.

The Ego self encourages us to look outside of ourselves for happiness and to fill the emptiness within. It sends us on an unending and often blind search for the next big thrill. This can come from the next hearty laugh, a night out with friends, a sexual encounter, financial success, fame from one's job or profession, a long-lasting relationship, or through the many other activities, interests, and experiences we pursue.

While all these things are fine and, in many cases, should be pursued to some degree — context and proportion are a big part of the degree to which they should be pursued — these things are not the true source of happiness. They are happiness illusions. When these illusions fade, and they always do, we continue our search — usually outside of ourselves — and look for more. We hunt for the next big thing to give us a jolt of positive and joyful energy. But the search is flawed. "Intent" is critical. Until we change our focus and look internally, we'll remain on an endless quest, seeking the next illusion to convince ourselves that we are happy, and perpetuate this tiresome cycle.

Sometimes, we do look within to fill the elusive goal of happiness. However, if we're looking to the intellect and not the Inner Selves, we may also encounter a problem. The brain and its thoughts are not external, like the previously mentioned examples.

They are inwardly focused. But the brain and its thoughts are not the source of happiness. Rather, they might be used to create a false sense of validation, which we then misinterpret as happiness. Two ways to do this immediately spring to mind.

The first will likely be something everyone will relate to: opinions. We all have opinions and often cling to them like a tired swimmer left alone in the middle of a vast ocean, clutching a life preserver to survive. Many times, sharing our opinions is an attempt to create external validation and acceptance from others. We're trying to fill the emptiness within, even if only temporarily. When others disagree with our opinion, we argue, valiantly defending our belief to the very end, as if it was a fundamental part of us. Why? To create or maintain the validation we initially sought when we first expressed the opinion. If there is no agreement, there is no validation and we're left where we began — seeking that validation to feel good about ourselves in that moment. Even worse, we may be forced to rethink our opinion, which can be a painful process.

The following is a quote from Dr. David R. Hawkins, MD, Ph.D. included in the book *Dissolving the Ego, Realizing the Self,* which is a compilation of some of Hawkins' teachings:

"All thought is vanity. All opinions are vanities. The pleasure of vanity is therefore the basis of the ego — unplug it and it collapses."

I read this quote many years ago but only recently came to truly understand its meaning. Our opinions have become lures for external validation, which the Ego self erroneously, but eagerly accepts as happiness. This particular confusion may have its roots in our early school years when we were given gold stars — admiration and positive support — for correctly answering a question about facts. We were rewarded for being "right." Unfortunately, we often conflate facts and opinions, but that's not what this is about. This is about allowing the Ego self to substitute external world validations and acceptance for real and continuing inner happiness.

Offering an opinion is like setting a trap in the wilderness, hoping to catch an unsuspecting animal to satisfy one's need for food. The Ego self is innocently trying to satisfy its hunger for Love and acceptance. Therefore, with the weight of the Ego self looming in the background, some forcefully offer their opinions, proclaiming their thoughts as 100 percent correct and declaring that all other viewpoints must be wrong. They intend to have others agree with their assessment of things and work diligently to change the minds of anyone who disagrees. Agreement is the validation they seek. Others take a subtler approach, stating their opinions in a much less threatening and gentle manner. They are more willing to respect the ideas of others and adjust accordingly. Although this may be indicative of a higher consciousness perspective, the initial motivation was likely the same. The goal is validation. To attain this, they desire agreement; to be judged by others as being right. They want the gold star.

This is the vanity of the Ego self. It is an attempt to bring attention to oneself with the hope that this will bring respect, honor, or even self-love and fill the emptiness within. Offering an opinion is a misguided attempt to create happiness. It's a placebo that, at best, can only create temporary joy or a momentary thrill, but not real happiness.

Another internal method the Ego self uses to create the illusion of happiness is with our thoughts themselves. Have you ever found yourself occupied by your thoughts, perhaps stuck in a continual thought loop about things you desire, or replaying in your mind an argument you had or might want to have in the future?

The first thing to understand is the brain and the mind are not the same. We will discuss this in more depth in the next chapter.

For now, please keep in mind that the brain is purely physical. It is an organ within the physical body that ceases to function when the body dies. The Ego self, even though it is a non-physical Spiritual aspect of ourselves, is purely physical in its orientation. Its only frame of reference is the body and the physical world. So, it should not be surprising that the Ego self attaches itself to the brain and seeks to control the brain's activities and focus. Left unchecked, the Ego self will commandeer the brain and use this powerful tool to control our lives by creating an endless supply of extraneous chatter in the form of thoughts and internal conversations. All these are distractions from our true Spiritual nature.

This is why many people have trouble meditating when they first begin. I often hear people say they cannot meditate because they cannot quiet the mind and its continual stream of thoughts. There is confusion in this statement: It's not the *mind* that needs quieting, it's the *brain*, and this is an example of the Ego self taking control. It doesn't want you to meditate, perhaps even fears it because it knows that one of the functions of meditation is to learn how to disconnect the Ego self from the brain. It doesn't want this to happen as commandeering the brain to create internal chatter is a powerful strategy the Ego self uses to maintain its control over our lives. With diligence, this can be overcome.

I ride a bicycle for exercise almost every day. I began riding about fifteen years ago when an orthopedic surgeon told me my knees were in good shape and would likely stay that way if I stopped running for exercise. I took his advice and took up cycling.

I usually experience two types of internal states when I ride. The first is meditative. I often reach a calm, quiet state, and create a deep connection with my God Self. I'll then have extensive conversations with it where I may or may not receive guidance and wisdom but always benefit from the interaction and companionship. In fact, this particular chapter for this book became significantly more detailed due to the revelations I received during one such ride. I did have the same type of interactive communication experiences with my God Self when I was running for exercise. In fact, it was a bit easier, as cycling does require a bit more external awareness.

During other bike rides, however, I sometimes encounter a totally different and unwanted internal state — a state of angst or even anger. To avoid these, and to keep any unwanted consequences in check, I must monitor myself diligently. Otherwise, these internal states can overtake any good feelings my bike rides bring, and they'll change my internal energies from positive to negative. This is an example of how runaway thoughts can override the desire and search for internal peace which, in addition to exercise, is always my goal for each bike ride.

Here's one scenario to illustrate this: Sometimes, as I pedal my bike through the streets of my neighborhood, I encounter real-world problems created by the many decisions our local government has made. Many of these have negatively impacted our area's quality of life. (The local government here does not operate for the greatest good of all.) In fact, some of their decisions have created very real and unnecessary inconveniences and actual dangers for the community and its residents. Many of these problems have worsened over time due to increases in population density and traffic. Since I always ride the same route, I see these things almost every day.

When negative thoughts about things like this are created, they can be accompanied by an unwanted bonus: the internal energy of anger. Perhaps you have experienced this type of self-created, anger energy too? With internal awareness, you become consciously aware of this energy and can feel it spread through the body in a wave. Often, anger energy will settle in the solar plexus and chest area and may even create a warm and flushed face for some. If you are familiar with this emotionally based, physical response, you know it's not a great feeling. No one truly wants to feel this way, though some have become so accustomed to this state of being that they mistakenly find a false sense of comfort when consumed by it.

It is useful to realize that the energy of anger is created by the Ego self. It employs a string of various thoughts, using them as tools to build and expand this distracting and destructive force. While it is natural for anger energy to arise, there is no need for it to become consuming, overwhelming, distracting. By employing internal awareness, you can remain in control. You can contextualize this energy to bring a better sense of proportion and perspective as well as the option to deny its attempt to take control of your decisions and actions. That is higher consciousness living, which is everyone's goal. Without this awareness, this contrary energy can fill the body and overtake the subtler, higher consciousness energies we'd all prefer to feel. It is then free to negatively influence our thoughts and actions and can become a downward spiral of unpleasantness. This is an example of how unchecked thoughts continuously rolling through the brain in an endless loop can become an inner distraction — which is the goal of the Ego self. It wants to distract you from the inner comfort and peace offered by the True Self. It wants to disconnect you from the positive energies of higher consciousness and from any possible communion with the God Self within.

Ultimately, being a slave to the erratic whims of the Ego self is not a good state of existence. In addition to the impact the above scenario will have on your current internal state of being, these types of negative states also can affect your future. When you focus on a particular energy state, good or bad, you strengthen and perpetuate its existence and power. It then projects outward from you and into the universe, which always responds by sending additional opportunities to experience more of the same. Like attracts like. You receive what you project. You reap what you sow.

More interesting, and perhaps confusing for many, the internal process just described is how the Ego self attempts to create happiness. It actually believes that this sort of negative thought loop is great. I realize this may seem contradictory — an association between a negative thought loop and happiness — but the Ego self gains its happiness in comfort, whether the comfort is real or a mere projection or interpretation of what it *believes* comfort should be. Remember, the Ego self is only comfortable when it is in control. It is in control when it teams up with the brain to run an unchecked program of circular thoughts that create feelings, even feelings of anger. This sense of control brings comfort to the Ego self and this comfort is erroneously substituted for, and often accepted as, happiness, even though the energy of anger is contrary to happiness and is an innately uncomfortable and undesirable state in which to live.

The remedy I employ to overcome these distracting and negative thought loops is the previously mentioned awareness. Inner awareness. Awareness of the physical body and the nature and substance of any feelings within. The power of awareness cannot be overstated, and it is immediately available to everyone, though using it effectively does take practice and diligence. I continually monitor myself. I feel. I focus on my internal state of being. Whenever I get into one of these loops, even though at this point in my life they seldom approach the all-consuming and ultra-apparent energy of anger, they're usually accompanied by some type of uncomfortable feeling within my body, usually a discomfort — almost like butterflies — in my solar plexus area. Although this feeling might be mild and subtle, it's still there. It is up to me to *feel* it.

This simple recognition and acknowledgment is a very powerful first step. Feeling any subtle discomfort or contrary energy in my body is a signal that my Ego self and its thoughts may be running out-of-control and I must intervene. This basic awareness is often enough to regain control, but I also take one more step. I make a conscious effort to change the energy by focusing on something positive. This brings good feelings within and changes my internal energy field from negative discomfort, to something positive and comfortable. In addition to the beneficial consequences in the immediate moment, it also has a longer-term impact. This newly created positive energy then projects outward and will reflect back to me in the future.

I can sum up the above scenario with just one word, which we have already explored in this chapter: validation. The Ego self is constantly looking for validation. It wants to matter and, more importantly, it wants others to believe and agree that it matters. Internal anger lets it feel like it is in control, and control is a form of validation. Validation also means that it matters — that it has value — and is often the real motivation behind the actions we take and the decisions we make. This motivational energy may be buried deep within, beneath layers of repressed memories of both good and bad experiences. Hidden though it may be, the desire for external validation is often the driving force pushing us to work so hard, especially to control our environment and surroundings and to manipulate others' perceptions of us. Those who are driven by the Ego self just want to be noticed and acknowledged. They want to matter in some way. They want to feel good, no matter how fleeting that good feeling is. What they really want is Love, but they're looking for it outside, rather than inside.

We've all experienced a "braggart," the person who continually points to what they've done and how much better and valuable they believe their accomplishments to be. This is the Ego self actively expressing its insecurities and fears. It brings to the forefront the lower consciousness internal state to which that individual identifies, which they then express outwardly. This is an extreme example of the Ego self and its search for outer-world validation, and most people are not burdened with this level of inner confusion and discomfort. However, almost everyone, to some degree, is looking for the same validation.

There is no point in judging ourselves or others for braggadocios behavior. It is more useful to accept things as they are; to allow them to be. This is Love. When we see these behaviors in others or discover them in ourselves, it is always better to think or project loving thoughts, both to others and to yourself. Thoughts, even unspoken ones, are energy that will register within you and in them, even if it's at the deepest levels, beyond conscious awareness. Those loving thoughts and energies may not cause an immediate advance in consciousness. However, they will register and create a stirring within, potentially awakening feelings that may lead to a different path, a better way.

This is especially true when holding this sort of Love for ourselves. Accepting who we are at any moment in time is a big part of Loving ourselves, even when we've done things we might later regret. We can always strive to do better next time. This is a strategy that will yield results. Forgiveness is a powerful technique. It is not for the benefit of others, as many believe. Forgiveness does not need to be shared. It is only for ourselves. It changes our internal energies for the better.

Love people. Love yourself. Love your brothers and sisters and all living things. This is the best each of us can do. And, as we will see in a coming chapter, this is how to Love your God Self. This is the true form of worship. Remember, visiting a "place of worship" is never necessary for anything other than social gatherings and community experience. These do have value, but they never need be part of one's Spiritual experience.

Let's take a deeper look at some other ways people create the illusion of inner peace and happiness. Sex is a good example. Sex is a strong drive for many and is perfectly natural. Some of us, though, become obsessed with sex, especially those in their twenties and thirties when the body is filled with powerful, sex-inducing hormones. Sex can be exciting and fun, and I'm not here to judge the behavior or say it's wrong. In fact, sex can be essential to our body's overall well-being. But, when one chooses to participate in sex as an activity, it should be done with an awareness of the internal motivators that sit behind the urge. Is it coming from a place of joy and genuine experience? Or is it coming from another part of you, the part seeking validation and acceptance to fill the inner void?

Contrary to what some religions would have you believe, from a truly Spiritual perspective, sex is not a bad or shameful thing. It feels good for the body and mind, which is why we like it and want more of it. The downside of sex is that it can be used as a substitute for inner peace and happiness. For some people, sex is the ultimate placebo to create the illusion of happiness. It can become an obsession and even an addiction. When it gets to that point, it becomes a distraction, which is probably the original reason sex was given a bad reputation thousands of years ago by some religions. They likely were trying to warn followers of the potential distraction. Unfortunately, in some religions, this reputation was expanded beyond this narrow scope and persists today to include any sex, regardless of internal motivations. Like any illusion, though, when looked at through unfocused eyes that may see it for something other than what it is, problems can arise.

The essence and energy that many would call "God" certainly doesn't attach any negative connotations to sex. Why would God do that? Sex is the way we procreate. If we didn't procreate, human life on Earth would cease to exist, and human life is one way that God experiences and grows through the universe's continuing expansion. Additionally, sex can be a physical expression of Love and Love is the most powerful energy in the universe, so how can God consider it to be a negative?

The Ego self always wants to experience physical pleasures, whatever they may be. It also wants to avoid pain and suffering. In addition to sex, drugs, and alcohol, which the Ego self perceives as pleasurable, many other experiences, desires, and activities also fit the "pleasurable" category. These can span a broad spectrum, from food and eating, to extreme and dangerous thrill-seeking activities like BASE jumping, which create feelings of joy and satisfaction for some. Ultimately, though, all these things are just experiences. One of the Ego self's jobs is to push us to try new and different things, to experience more. New experiences enhance our individual lives and through those experiences the greater consciousness of all also expands. Engaging in pleasurable things, like sex, is certainly part of life and is to be experienced. It and other experiences only become problems if one is overly driven by their urges — whatever they may be — to the degree that one's judgment "clouds" and they're distracted from the Spiritual world within.

If sex does become a prevailing thought, and one becomes overly invested in satisfying only the physical aspects of self — the body and its needs (sex or otherwise) — this will create an imbalance. This imbalance tilts the Individualized Self to control by the Ego self, to the detriment of the True Self.

Again, sex is just one example of basic pleasure. I used it as an example because most will find it relatable. But the imbalance described above can be created with every type of pursuit, even the ultimate pursuit: renewing and strengthening the connection to the True Self, the God Self — the search for enlightenment.

If one commits so deeply to this pursuit, and it is done to the exclusion of everything else — as noble as this might seem — an imbalance might be created. And, as is the case with all internal imbalances, the potential to lose connection to the True Self increases, which is the complete opposite of what one is trying to accomplish with a search for consciousness and enlightenment. The original intent of any goal, even an entirely altruistic goal like higher consciousness, can be pushed to the background and buried beneath the energy of pure desire, potentially transforming the work toward this goal to become more of a distraction. This, too, is a strategy often employed by the Ego self. So, even the pursuit of Spiritual growth — higher consciousness and enlightenment — can be problematic when it is out of balance with other aspects of life. The Ego self is deceptively creative as it ruthlessly works to satisfy its desires and maintain control.

Those who are not completely consumed by just one thing also need to beware; the Ego self can employ the same type of trap using a combination of several things to distract us from our Inner Selves. One example of this might be drinking alcohol to excess in combination with sex. Experience shows that this is relatively common for younger adults. Bad? Not necessarily. But might awareness of the motivations behind these choices be beneficial? Absolutely.

Another factor to consider: These distracting pursuits are not limited to either the physical or the non-physical. These, too, can be combined. An example of a pursuit that combines both the physical and the non-physical is being consumed with the goal of making money, and one's job. The non-physical component is the single-minded focus on making and accumulating wealth, or prestige from a job. The physical component is the actual work done to achieve this goal. There are many stories of people obsessed with success and money. They become workaholics, working twenty hours a day, every day. Whether they failed or succeeded is not relevant here. Nor is it wrong or bad to want success. The point is the motivating factor, the driving force within, the underlying intent. Why are they acting this way? Anything that becomes all-consuming, to the exclusion of other aspects of life, can be enough to create an internal imbalance, which leads one away from the True Self, and into the waiting arms of the Ego self. Vanity, exercise, and weight loss is another example of this potentially destructive and distracting physical/non-physical combination.

In fact, for most, it's usually not just one thing that creates these sorts of inner imbalances and distractions. It's more likely to be a combination of things, like a job, a partner, and family. Then, add a hobby or another activity to this mix and the likelihood of becoming distracted, of shifting focus away from the Inner Selves, becomes difficult to avoid. Outer world pursuits tend to direct our focus outside of ourselves, away from our Inner Selves. This doesn't mean that these experiences and activities should be avoided. We *should* do them. They just need to be pursued *consciously* — properly contextualized and kept in their proper proportion. They're just things, activities, or experiences to be temporarily enjoyed by both the Ego self and the True Self. They are not identities, nor should we allow them to overwhelm our awareness of the Inner Selves.

Life and outer-world experiences do tend to lead us away from our Inner Selves. The loving inner aspect of *us* — the True Self — gets overlooked or even lost while the outer physical world and the Ego self gets all the attention. We all experience this to some degree, lured and cajoled by either the physical or the intellectual treasures found in this world. But these things are meaningful and useful. We are here to experience them. These experiences are tools of the God Self, which is part of the Greater God, enabling its expansion. So, how does one escape the trap of distraction created by life's experiences? Context, proportion, and awareness, with awareness being the critical factor. It opens the door to context and proportion. Awareness of the messages you receive from within, which often come in the form of *feelings* and can be communications from the God Self, is the bridge to a better understanding of your *Selves* and reality.

Even though our daily activities and life experiences may not be harmful physically, emotionally, or even intellectually, there's always a risk that they can take on addictive qualities and distract us from the quiet and understated True Self. This happens even though they may never be taken to the extremes associated with the more traditional types of harmful addiction. Drugs, for example, may first come to mind when considering forms of addiction. But from a Spiritual perspective, other addictive behaviors can be just as harmful. For example, food is an addiction to some, and its consequences can sometimes be visible. Even seemingly healthy things like exercise can become addictions. In fact, almost anything pursued to the point of inner distraction can be an addiction, including one's work, music, thrill-seeking, sex, and more. As activities and experiences, none of these are inherently problematic. It is only when they are used to fill the void within, to create the illusion of happiness and distract and separate us from our True Self, that they become a problem.

Of course, crossing the line from experience, to simple distraction, and then to full-blown addiction is the worst-case scenario. All things can be experienced without sinking to that level of harm. It is perfectly acceptable and even beneficial to experience the many aspects and activities our world offers. Delicious food, fulfilling sex, and even recreational drugs are all okay when experienced in proper context: Simply as experiences and nothing more. Experience is why we're all here. It is only through experience that we learn, grow, and gain wisdom. Knowledge is an intellectual pursuit and can be acquired through research and study. But wisdom comes from the *heart* and can only be acquired through experience when combined with self-examination and analysis. Wisdom is an everyday adventure and is a positive byproduct of awareness.

When it comes to the choices we make — which determine our experiences — in addition to context and proportion, motivation also is an important factor. Living life proportionately and from a more balanced, *well intentioned* perspective enables us to remain connected to, and in contact with, the True Self aspect of the Individualized Self. Examination of your intentions from a place of extreme self-awareness and honesty is the key to understanding your true motivations — the driving force behind the choices you make and the actions you take.

There is another type of addiction that overtakes some people: codependence. From a clinical perspective, codependence and addiction might be viewed differently. From a Spiritual perspective, they are the same. Codependence is an attempt to fill the void created by a disruption in our connection to the True Self. We all want to feel this connection. We crave the Love, contentment, acceptance, and inner peace it brings. When these wonderful internal feelings are absent, we can connect to another person as a substitute for feeling connected to ourselves.

Humans have invented many things to fill what we wrongly perceive as an empty container of Love within. Here are two more examples that might seem completely unrelated, but are very much the same: patriotism and overly enthusiastic sports fans. When I say "overly enthusiastic sports fans," I refer to those who find a significant part of their identity in a specific team or sport. Many people here in the USA attend sporting events dressed in elaborate costumes, including face and body paint, helmets, modified shoulder pads (to football games), and other props. They go to every home game, and perhaps even some away games, always dressed in these very decorative costumes, some of which likely take several hours to get into.

I would guess that some of these people would readily acknowledge that they have created an identity for themselves, an "alter-ego." Some, though, maybe even most, do not realize that they're doing this to feel better about themselves. It fills an inner desire for acknowledgment and recognition. They seek external validation and wrap themselves in the persona of their team. If the team wins... great. They excitedly exclaim things like "We won!" and "We're number one!" However, the truth is, many of these sports enthusiasts have never even played the sport, either in the street as children with their friends, or in a more organized way. So, the idea that "we won" — signifying that they are somehow a part of a championship team — is an illusion. They are not *really* part of the team. But they latch onto that idea, believing they have accomplished something great, even though all they did was spectate. It brings them a false sense of validation, momentary joy, and a way to differentiate and project an identity to the world.

Patriotism is similar. Rather than identify with a team, though, some people attempt to elevate their stature by attaching themselves to their country, wrapping themselves in a flag, and often drawing battle lines to discern what constitutes a "good" or "bad" citizen. They try to decide what's "right" and "wrong" about and for the country. This particular construct is the same as the sports fanatic. There is nothing real there, but they feel better about themselves, especially when they attempt to elevate themselves above others by applying a litmus test based on their opinions and ideologies, which *they* deem "patriotic."

Both sports fanaticism and patriotism are just additional examples of how the Ego self creates distractions to provide a false sense of happiness and temporary relief from the oppressive void within. There are many more. The Ego self can be ingenious in its deceptions. We all feel an urge within to fill this void. Unfortunately, most of us look in the wrong place, which can spawn codependence, addiction, and these other behaviors and issues.

Back in the 1980s, a song was part of the soundtrack to the movie, *Urban Cowboy.* The song was named "Lookin' for Love." The hook for the song was the lyric: "I was lookin' for love in all the wrong places... " That's what many of us do. We look outside ourselves for something to fill the void within. When we find something that seems to do the job, like a new relationship or friend, a career, or even food or drugs, we can become codependent; addicted. We believe it is the best we can do. By now, it should come as no surprise that these substitutes are not the best we can do.

The emptiness many people feel and the yearning for something better can be overcome by reconnecting with the True Self, by building a bridge back to this source of everything.

All the things I have described here occur within the realm of the Individualized Self, untouched by the influence of the God Self. We are free to choose, experience, and be whatever we desire. We are free to either choose the True Self or not.

It is important to know that, if you let it, the God Self will do its best to create and manifest all your dreams and desires — the choices arrived at by the Individualized Self — whatever they may be. It does not matter if they are perceived as good or evil. There is no judgment. That's why evil exists in our world and often seems to proliferate. The God Self works for us to help us create any and all of the desires we focus on, including those things society would collectively deem bad, wrong, and evil. Some call this the Law of Attraction. Regardless of the label applied, though, it is real and works without judgment. Because there is no judgment, we are free to create; this is free will and choice in action. What actually manifests, what you create, is a function of your ability to follow through and to receive the creation. This, too, is not the same for everyone.

It is we who use our free will and choice to create the so-called "bad" and "evil" in the world. Evil stems from the Ego self. The Individualized Self makes our choices. But when decisions are made by default, completely influenced by the Ego self and un-challenged and unchecked by the True Self, evil can result. Again, our God Self does not judge the choices and decisions made by the Individualized Self. That is its scope of responsibility. The God Self just responds without judgement to these choices and desires, whatever they may be. This is why personal responsibility for your thoughts and actions is critical to your well-being, and to our world. Your thoughts and choices do matter, even those that you believe might be small and trivial.

So, if you want a better life for yourself and want to see a better world, monitor yourself. Feel your body and pay attention to your thoughts. An out-of-control brain, continually rehash-ing unhelpful thoughts, is a challenge to well-being. This type of brain tends to collaborate with the Ego self and, in addition to being an immediate source of sadness and self-created misery, it also has long-term effects on your life. It does have creative power. The negative thoughts one thinks today, right now, can create more negative situations in the future. This can lead to even more negative thoughts and negative situations, which results in more difficult and unpleasant experiences. The cycle can become self-perpetuating.

The Ego self connects to the brain. It usurps this powerful tool and tries to keep it for itself. Quieting your brain will benefit you. Meditation is a good tool to learn this skill. Left unchecked, the brain/Ego self collaboration can lead to a spiral downward. For some, this will seem like an endless cycle of disappointment, sadness, and the feeling of being unloved and alone.

Although the Individualized Self is a big part of who you are, it is not all that you are. You have a God Self within. We'll get to that aspect of you in an upcoming chapter. The Individualized Self is changeable. It can be molded. You can apply internal awareness to contextualize it with Love and bring proper balance between the Ego self and the True Self. This is a roadmap for life, a schematic of the Individualized Self. Having this understanding and developing an awareness of the inner you will help you make better choices as life moves forward to create a better life and a more loving world.

8

The Mind, the Brain, and Distractions

I n the last chapter, I mentioned the Ego self's desire to take control of the brain. This collaboration between the Ego self and the brain can have serious consequences. Ultimately, the distractions it creates can imprison you in the past or the future. Either way, you are taken from the present moment, which is the only thing that matters. The present is the only thing that is real. Without internal awareness to help you recognize and stop this self-destructive behavior, you become a victim of this cunning scheme orchestrated by the Ego self.

One effective tactic the Ego self uses to occupy the brain is to rehash past conversations or arguments you've had with others. When reliving these incidents, though, the Ego self usually wants to create a different outcome.

Let's take a look at one example to illustrate this Ego self/brain alliance. Have you ever had an argument or disagreement that didn't turn out the way you would have liked? If so, did you have trouble leaving this experience in the past and forgetting about it? Did you find yourself replaying this argument over and over in your head, imagining all the things you didn't say that might have created a different outcome?

Reliving the past locks your focus onto pointless, circular discussions and arguments about events that likely have no real importance to the current moment. Dwelling in the past or future draws your attention and focus away from the present moment and has the additional effect of minimizing or even completely negating any higher aspects of the Self, which may be trying to communicate with you. It steals your inner joy and disrupts any sense of inner peacefulness. This is another way the Ego self maintains control, making us and our brain its servants, rather than having this control in the hands of a balanced Individualized Self, enabling us to have the choice to employ the Ego self and the brain to serve at our discretion.

Let's try a little experiment. Try to think back to the last time you found yourself stuck in a loop when you thought about and replayed a conversation over and over again. If nothing comes to mind, no problem. Just do your best.

If you have something in mind, was it an argument or a heated discussion with someone? Or was it a lighter conversation? I want you to think about that right now. Concentrate on that discussion and try to relive that past moment. Take yourself back to the time when you were having this conversation. See it vividly in your mind and try to make it real for yourself, as if it were happening again right now. (I realize this may be uncomfortable but please try anyway. The discomfort, if any, will pass quickly as soon as you let it.)

If you are able to get yourself back to that time, this time try to take note of how your body feels. Do you have any uneasiness in your chest or stomach areas? Do these sensations feel familiar? Are they similar to how your body felt back when this thought-loop originally transpired, back when you first rehashed this conversation in your brain? Does it feel good (light, free, joyful)? Or does it feel dense (heavy, burdened, tense)?

If the event you're recalling was something upsetting, I presume the feelings were more disturbing: dense, heavy, burdened, and/or tense. As you relive this past experience, realize that you are feeling this way again, right now, just from recalling the situation. If you are able to take your awareness of that unsettling feeling to even deeper levels within, you might also find that you didn't (and perhaps still don't) feel very good about yourself and your life at that point. If this is what you were feeling, you were in a state of discomfort and not a state of happiness. This is an example of the destructive fallout that can be created by a collaboration between the Ego self and the brain.

Now, it's time to end this exercise. Take a deep breath and slowly exhale. Repeat this a few times until the events you've remembered fade away and you feel yourself and your thoughts return to the present.

Happiness is not about an event. It is a state of being and it comes from within. Regardless of outer-world circumstances, you always have the power and the ability to feel happy. If you monitor yourself (internal awareness), whenever you realize that you are feeling energy within that is something other than happiness, you can change it. You are a creator. Create the energy you'd rather feel; it's a conscious choice you can make at any time. Simply choose to make a change. The Ego self tries to make this difficult, but you can bypass it. Use the breathing exercise described above to relax your brain and body. That is the better choice. When you remain stuck in a negative thought loop constructed by the Ego self, succumbing to the often-seductive allure found in these distractions and ideas, you leave behind the input from your True Self.

Awareness of these internal struggles and processes is a way out of the loveless void and back to happiness. With awareness comes choice and control. A situation cannot be addressed until you recognize it exists. Pay attention to the internal signals your body sends. This is the foundation of internal awareness.

Now, let's take the above example to another level. What about a scenario when you're stuck in one of these thought-loops and you encounter someone who has nothing to do with that particular loop? Since this new person arrived on the scene while you were already upset — and therefore not in the mood to be a loving, positive person — you treat this person in an inappropriate way. You've now pushed some of your bad feelings on them, perhaps ruining their day, thus increasing the negative energy in our world. Is this fair, especially considering this new person had done nothing to deserve being the recipient of your negative energy?

The overall effect of a scenario such as this is that the feelings generated by replaying the prior disagreement you've had with someone else has now involved an unsuspecting, innocent person, and has overtaken your sense of the current moment. This is living in the past, which no longer exists, at the expense of the present, the only thing that is real, and perfectly sets the stage for the next present moment to be a negative one. These negative loops can be self-perpetuating.

The above may be an overt or extreme illustration of how this complex relationship works. I used it because it should be relatable to most people and demonstrates how the Ego self takes control of our brains, our choices, and our lives. We let our brains run wild — unchecked — continually thinking about *this* or *that*, sometimes obsessively replaying past experiences or future desires over and over in an attempt to find satisfaction, joy, validation, and Love. The truth is, we all just want to feel good about life and ourselves.

However, continually replaying past events or spending your valuable energy focusing on future possibilities is wasting valuable creative energies on illusions. These are the placebos discussed in the previous chapter. The past no longer exists, and the future is yet to be created. This sort of mental activity will not yield the inner state of happiness we all seek. In fact, it is a distraction, removing us from the present moment, the only thing that is real, and takes us someplace else. Our real power and creative energies reside in the present, in *now*, not in the past. The present moment is the only true reality we have.

When not firmly planted in the soil of the present, you are more likely to miss the messages and guidance from your True Self. This guidance always comes in the now, and might never be repeated, so it is best to practice awareness and keep your focus in the present. Time spent replaying the past or dreaming about the future in a prolonged loop of thought increases the likelihood that you'll miss an important communication, a bit of life-changing, internal guidance that the True Self might be attempting to share with you.

Many get stuck in these sorts of thought loops without even realizing this. When these loops revolve around good things, they can bring good feelings. Since we're all just trying to feel good, this may seem harmless and actually can be beneficial. However, they're still illusions and can become addicting. Like all addictions, the bad usually outweighs the good, especially when the good is a construct of an Ego self/brain collaboration. The value these may have is in their potential to create future situations with more good feelings. This is a positive consequence. But beware: becoming lost in the past or the future to feel better is addictive and the danger lies in opting for this, rather than just feeling the inner Love available in every present moment. Collaborations between the brain and the Ego self usually don't end well. They usually create a false sense of reality that crumbles with time.

The Ego self likes to stay in its comfort zone. It doesn't like change and often struggles against new things. To stay in its comfort zone, it needs the illusion of control over you and your Individualized Self and often uses deception as a mechanism to maintain its dominance. Its perspective, identity, and the source of its power is fear. But even the Ego self doesn't want to feel fear, so it attempts to ignore the associated feeling, even if only temporarily, by establishing and maintaining a sense of control. The deep-seated internal foundation of fear, however, can be permanently overcome through a process of internal awareness and introspection, which includes acknowledging, loving, and then releasing the underlying and often hidden causes of this fear. It is up to you to be the director, to take back control. That is a choice you can make. The Individualized Self is the director and should control the Ego self, not the other way around. You are the Individualized Self, though it may not seem that way to you now.

When you allow the Ego self to take control, you willingly give away your true power and then live with the consequences of its decisions. True, you probably do this with good intentions. You have a strong internal desire to feel happiness and Love, to feel comfortable with yourself and your world, and you see this as the best way. However, as previously noted, the Ego self does not provide these things, even though it works continually with the brain to convince us that it does. And most of us do fall into this trap, which is why our lives and the world can, at times, descend into chaos.

Throughout history, many people of lower consciousness have taken power, either through valid elections or by force. But we cannot put all blame on them. These people are a societal mirror, an outer-world manifestation of our collective inner fears. These folks do their best to stoke fear in others as that is their own natural, internal state and they want everyone to feel the same. This is how they maintain their control, just as the Ego self does within each individual.

When our leaders are higher consciousness individuals, they act as a positive "check" on the lower consciousness energies others can project. In the absence of these checks, which help to balance all of us, the outer world can descend into a less harmonious expression of reality. It will always reflect the current dominant state of the collective inner consciousness of humankind. The world is a mirror, showing us who we really are on the inside.

The reflection of the Inner Selves we see in the outer world is not a punishment. Rather, it's a call to awareness. It is beckoning to us, asking us to do a better job to ignite our inner awareness. Developing a deeper understanding of and connection to the Inner Selves enables us to make better choices, both individually and collectively as a community. If we all did better — each one of us making a real effort to get to know our Inner Selves — more of our choices would be made with full awareness of the internal Spiritual anatomy we all share. Then, we'd make better choices for our own lives and for issues that shape the world. Ultimately, this would then reflect back to us in the mirror that is our collective outer-world reality. Life would be better and more beautiful for everyone.

Earlier, I promised to get back to the mind and how it differs from the brain. The brain is the organ located inside your skull. It consists of nerve cells, synapses, chemical processes, and a whole lot more. The mind, however, isn't in your physical body at all. It exists outside of you. It's a non-physical entity to which we're all connected through the *heart*. The mind exists on and across many dimensions, most of which we are not consciously aware of. It also can be called the collection of consciousness and can be accessed by the Individualized Self.

The mind is a collection of every thought, idea, and action created in the universe. Most real solutions, discoveries, new inventions, and wisdom come from the mind. Revolutionary technologies come from the mind. Great art, great music, and great poetry come from the mind. While it is true that the brain might be involved in helping us process, understand, focus on, create, and fine-tune these things, this isn't where they begin. The brain is not the source, it is the medium. These concepts originate in the mind.

The brain is programmed like a computer. Improper programming leads to poor and incorrect (bad) data. If we input false or corrupt information, the output must also be bad or corrupted. Bad data can lead to poor choices and decisions. The Ego self is very much aware of this. It thrives in this type of environment and works every day to create chaos within by attempting to commandeer the impressionable brain, which has trouble discerning truth from falsehood. It then manipulates us to believe what it wishes, simply to serve its purpose — to feel validated — regardless of whether the information it wants us to believe is based in reality. This is the source of so much of the pain and suffering we see in our own lives and our world.

You may have read or studied the Rudyard Kipling poem, "If: A Father's Advice to His Son." When thinking about the Ego self and its use of the brain, the first line seems to sum it up perfectly: "If you can keep your head when all about you are losing theirs…" One might think this is about panic or stressful situations. I believe his point was referring to the Ego self and its use of the brain to control our behaviors. Most of us are not "keeping our head." Too often, our thoughts are all over the place, being held hostage by what is typically a random and oppositional Ego self. It is important to overcome this.

There is an alternative. It is possible to disconnect the Ego self from the brain and to quiet all this distracting, internal chatter. When you achieve this, you will start to experience inner peace. A useful tool to help find your inner peace is meditation and, particularly, breathing exercises, which can be used to enter a meditative state. Over time and with practice, meditation will reduce the excess brain activity driven by the Ego self, allowing a new calmness and quiet to emerge. This calm is the essence and energy of the True Self, to which we are always connected. And, from this calm, you will begin to catch glimpses of the God Self, allowing a new reality and truth to seep into your life.

Visualizations during meditation can also be very helpful. These can be likened to directives from the True Self to occupy the brain; to keep it busy with more useful activities than the useless, distracting chatter many experience. Give the brain a project and it will comply. That's its function. When visualizations are directed to your inner world, you begin to regain control of your brain and internalize your focus and perspective, where they need to be. It's a win-win! If you'd like to learn the simple, yet powerful breathing technique and visualizations I have successfully used for many years to feel the internal essence of my God Self, please click the link below, or type the following URL into your browser: https://brucebernstein.me/extras-discovering-your-god-self/.

In addition to ending the excessive chatter created by the brain and ceasing its collaboration with the Ego self, there's another aspect to consider. As you were reading about the mind earlier in this chapter, you may have thought: "It would be great if I had access to all the knowledge and wisdom you mentioned." It is available to you and it's all about a connection to the mind through the True Self.

First, know that you're already connected to the mind. But what you really need is on-demand, conscious access. You can achieve this by developing internal awareness of the different aspects of the Self and gaining the ability to quiet the brain and its false master, the Ego self. This will give you a more conscious access to the True Self. Your True Self has a direct connection to the God Self, which is directly connected to the mind. In fact, it is the mind. The Ego self does not have the same connection to the God Self, though it is connected, but it will claim responsibility for any and all knowledge and wisdom received from this unlimited source.

It may sound like a lot, but it's not that difficult. A conscious connection to the True Self is supposed to be an instinctive part of our existence, but we've forgotten about this powerful aspect of ourselves. Tapping into the mind to access its wisdom is natural once you establish a strong connection with the True Self and learn to focus on the answers you seek for the problems or questions you may have. It all boils down to awareness; inner awareness. Since you're already connected to the mind, you don't have to do anything but learn to recognize and actively utilize this connection to make it a valuable and powerful resource. It's really just a process of turning down the volume of the extraneous noise created by the Ego self, which we all see and hear in our everyday lives, and tuning into a higher level of consciousness — a more conscious day-to-day existence.

To clarify one crucial point: After becoming consciously aware of your connection to the source of everything and making your request for information, the answers you seek might not arrive immediately — it might take a little time. And that's okay. It's all part of the process. If you do experience a delay in receiving the answers you seek, you are not being punished. Nor is the delay an effort to make you beg or bargain for the information, as some do in their prayers. "Oh God," they may pray, "if you'll only give me this, then I promise to do better at that." This sort of negotiating is unnecessary and usually a waste of time and energy.

The delay is usually about one or more of these three things: 1) There will be times when you'll need to be prepared to receive the information, so you'll be able to recognize and understand it when it comes, which may involve some knowledge accumulation, or, 2) You may have some karmic obligations which must first be addressed, or, 3) You're not *really* listening, meaning you don't hear or recognize the guidance when it comes due to distractions — your brain is too preoccupied by the Ego self. The latter is most often the case for too many people, too much of the time.

The information will come if you are persistent in your desire and continue seeking. Control the brain, discover the mind.

As an example of the mind in action, much of the information you're reading in this book came from my connection to the mind through my God Self. The words are not necessarily from the mind, although some of the sentences and paragraphs are, but the concepts and ideas came from the mind. At this point in my life, I am not a very imaginative person. (This current limitation is changeable, as are all things.) Rather, my life has been directed toward gaining a more concrete understanding of universal truth and our Spiritual nature. These were my primary motivations.

My current state of imaginative capacity makes it extremely unlikely that I could have invented the things you're reading in this book. I'm not very creative in that way and imagination and fantasy are not what drive me. I also have no desire to share any information unless I know it to be based in absolute reality. I am entirely focused on bringing truth to the table with the highest degree of integrity and purity and have questioned everything I have learned with extreme diligence. During my lifelong search for answers, I never read or saw anything like the information presented in this book. It is true that some of the masters whose work I have read and studied did allude to some of the things presented here, but it was never explained or contextualized in this way — with the specifics and details that I'm sharing. So, where did it come from? This information was willingly shared with me, over time, through my connection to the mind.

In fact, the idea for these last few paragraphs only came to me today, December 16, 2020. I had just finished what I'd thought would be my final edit of this chapter (there have been far more edits than I'd ever expected) and left for my daily bike ride. As previously mentioned, my bike rides are semi-meditative states when I usually commune with my God Self. They are some of the most joyful times of my day and I look forward to them. I feel this joy despite the fact that during one of these rides I experienced the most traumatic event of my life. You'll read about that in Chapter 13, *Life After Death*. After years of practice, my brain quickly quiets during these rides without any active prompting, and I naturally fall into a deep connection to my God Self. Distractions fall away with the calming sound of the wind whistling through my helmet and past my ears and I am completely focused in the present moment. During today's ride, not long after I began peddling, the idea came to me to include this information as an example of how connection to the mind can work. I was not thinking about this, or anything else in the moment. My brain was quiet and clear, which allowed this information, this idea, to be communicated to me, to filter through in great detail.

Another example also came to me during this ride. Steve Jobs, the founder and former driving force behind Apple, brought new and wonderful inventions to life and changed the world. I do not know Mr. Jobs. Nor do I have any connection with him, other than the one connection to the collective consciousness we all share. But I do know that the ideas for some or all his inventions and creations and the challenges he overcame to create them did not come from his brain. They came from his connection to the mind. His brain, and the brain power contained in the intellectual capacities of those who assisted him with these projects certainly played a part in bringing these ideas to fruition. But the *ideas* for these inventions did not originate in the brain. They came from the mind. Only after they were received by Jobs was the brain engaged to help bring the idea from the ethereal realm to the physical world, where it changed and advanced our collective reality.

9

The God Self

Now we get to meat of the discussion, the most talked about and misunderstood aspect of Spirituality: God and the God Self. Everything you've already read in the prior chapters is part of this topic. The Individualized Self — along with its components, the Ego self and the True Self — are fundamental to any discussion about God. But people tend to view these aspects of ourselves as separate and distinct from one another, and from God. Ultimately, they are not.

As discussed, we have an Individualized Self, and this does give us a singular perspective from which to view our lives and the world. But the Individualized Self is part of the God Self, which is your individual portion of the Greater God. The Greater God encompasses everything. So based on that hierarchy, any discussions about the Ego self, the True Self, and the Individualized Self are, in fact, also discussions about God and the God Self.

I'm certain there are those reading this book who are confused by the above. It can be confusing. Then there are those who likely question the existence of God itself, wondering: Is there a God? What is God? Where is God? Can I talk to God? Will God talk to me? Will God help me? And on and on.

The answers to most of these questions become clear when another key question is explored: Is it possible for God to be inside us? Although a little cryptic, the answer to this critical question is simple. It is *impossible* for God to *not* be inside us.

To better understand this answer, it might be helpful to first discuss the aforementioned question: What is God? The answer to this also is simple: God is everything. I am not trying to be flippant with this answer. It's just the truth.

Think of a giant bakery filled with thousands of loaves of bread. On the surface, these all look the same, but underneath each is slightly different. Some are made from plain wheat flour, others from rye, whole wheat, and more, including gluten free. These foundational ingredients infuse each loaf with an energy, an essence — a distinct set of properties, knowledge, and instinctual behaviors.

The bakery is the universe — consciousness, or God — and each loaf represents a separate but equal portion of God. There's one loaf for dogs. One for elephants. One for ants. One for mosquitos. One for trees. One for humans, and so on. In fact, there's one loaf for each element of our universe, physical and non-physical, living and non-living, like dirt, water, air, and more.

Now, imagine that the one loaf representing humans has been sliced into billions of equal pieces. Each slice represents just one person, including those currently in physical bodies as well as those currently not experiencing physicality. Each of these slices is a God Self for that particular individual. These slices, though, are covered with layers of toppings and condiments, giving each slice a unique flavor. One slice is covered with strawberry preserves. Another with seedless blackberry. There's one covered with mustard and slices of turkey and one with scrambled eggs, cheese, and ketchup. The variations are infinite. For most, the choice of which topping to use are made primarily by the Ego self aspect of the Individualized Self.

These toppings represent the choices made by the Individualized Self and contribute to the creation of the personality — tastes, preferences, likes, and dislikes. Under all these toppings, though, we're all the same. We all originate from the same loaf of bread. That is consciousness or what is often termed the universe. I call this the Greater God.

God is the computer, the book, or the Kindle you're using to read this. It's the asphalt or concrete that makes up the roads you drive and the sidewalks you stroll. It's the grass, weeds, and trees; the entire animal, insect, and aquatic kingdoms; every particle in the universe; and yes, it includes all of humanity. God is consciousness, and consciousness is everything, living and non-living, physical and non-physical, seen and unseen.

However, not all consciousness is the same. There are different levels, or degrees, of consciousness. Dr. David R. Hawkins wrote extensively about this subject. His research attempted to quantify Spirituality and consciousness to help people better understand these abstract concepts and revealed the many levels, from the low to the very high, with many in between.

Some species are higher in consciousness than others. A dog registers a higher level of consciousness than does a lion. And, for any particular species — be it human, dog, cat, bees, or trees

— not all individuals within each species will exist at the same level of consciousness. There always will be differences. Some humans have reached the highest levels of consciousness possible here on planet Earth, such as the persons known as Jesus of Nazareth, Buddha, or Mahavatar Babaji, while others exist at low levels.

So, God is everywhere and is the foundation of everything and that includes you. In fact, if God were not already inside you, right now and always, you would not be alive. The God Self gave life to your body in this physical realm and is the essence and energy that enables you to continue living. When the God Self withdraws from the body, the body dies to become a lifeless object that slowly disintegrates over time. But the real you, the God Self and the True Self aspect of your Individualized Self, survives. Your portion of God — your slice of the loaf: the God Self within — will go on eternally, as will the True Self and the Individualized Self. Even though your current body ceases to exist, you continue along your path.

The core of your being is the essence and energy of the Greater God via the God Self. The God Self is your distinct and personal portion of the Greater God, which encompasses everything. Your God Self is both separate from, yet also part of, the entirety of everything. Consider a lone water molecule in the immense ocean. The ocean offers a life-giving environment supporting various creatures and plants, providing a comfortable home for both living things as well as inanimate objects like sand and rocks. This vast body of water is made up of many trillions of individual water molecules. Each individual molecule of water — H_2O — is separate and distinct. However, it has joined with others just like it to create the oceans. Although each molecule itself is water, a lone water molecule is not the ocean. To be an ocean, all its brother and sister molecules are required. Like the ocean, the Greater God is made up of all its many individual components.

Your God Self is only one of these individual components and, like an individual molecule of water, is an equal part of the bigger ocean. Your God Self is an all-encompassing but individualized portion of the Greater God. The God essence within, the God Self, is the spark of life. Without the God Self, your body would be a lifeless object. Your body is a "temple of God" and belongs to the God Self, not the Individualized Self.

Here's another interesting revelation. You are not the one looking out from your eyes and hearing with your ears. The Individualized Self is not the first to see, hear, taste, touch, and smell. It is the God Self that operates the five senses and is the first to experience all their inputs. It sees through your eyes and listens with your ears. Only after the God Self experiences the senses are these impressions then shared with the Individualized Self. This sharing is the one function where the God Self continually uses the communicator, sending these sensory experiences through it to the Individualized Self. Remember that the Individualized Self is not the real you, though it is the aspect to which you more easily align. The God Self is the real you and is here to grow through experience, and so it does. It experiences, and then, out of compassion for the Individualized Self, shares these experiences.

Your God Self is 100 percent devoted to you. It is you, so there is nothing else or no one else it needs to attend. It has no other responsibilities. It is there for you and only you, to work with you, help you, and to be you. Your job is to learn to be 100 percent open to, aware of, and dedicated to it.

Being 100 percent dedicated does not mean to bow down, worship, or even praise it. Remember that God and the God Self are never in need of worship or praise. Only the Ego self requires external validation. Being dedicated means you should build an internal relationship with the God Self and seek out and listen for its guidance, companionship, and Love. It is, however, okay to offer the energies of thanks and gratitude, but quietly and internally. Gratitude can facilitate the movement of communications from the Individualized Self, through the Communicator, and to the God Self, but is never sought by the God Self. It is your choice whether to use these energies, or not.

You are free to ignore your God Self, as most do — although I strongly advise you pay attention to it. Regardless, the God Self will always wait patiently for you to choose to reconnect with it. It is ready to share its companionship, Love, and wisdom and is instantly available to speak with you, guide you, and answer all your questions. However, you must initiate these communications. All you need to do is ask! It will not volunteer or impose information. To do so would be considered a trespass, a violation of the free will and choice all have been given.

So, through the lens of the bigger picture, we're all the same inside. We're made of the same stuff, physically and Spiritually. When you look at another individual, you're looking at God incarnate. When you're looking at an animal, plant, or even a building, you're looking at God.

The differences between people are the product of the Individualized Self. The gift of free will and choice resides within the Individualized Self. It is up to that aspect of you, and its two components — the Ego self and the True Self — to mold your tastes, preferences, thoughts, and tendencies. These are what make each of us different. But underneath all these layers of desire and experience is the same energy and essence: the God Self.

The Individualized Self is a derivative of the God Self. The Ego self and the True Self both are created by your God Self. The

True Self is eternal, but the Ego self is created at the time of birth for each incarnation and dies with the body. Free will, choice and autonomy are gifts given by the God Self to the Individualized Self. This allows you to develop your own personality, the source of our differences, and offers a couple of benefits.

First, our differences make the world a far more interesting place. Life would be terribly boring and redundant if we were all exactly the same all the time. Differences are a wonderful gift enabled by our free will and choice.

The second benefit may seem like it is intended for us, and it does add value and interest to our lives and the world, but it's really more for the God Self. This benefit is growth and learning through experiences. The goal of the God Self is to experience. God is always expanding, growing, learning, and increasing its consciousness to greater levels. Growth and change are constant. We waste so much time and energy resisting growth and change but, as the Borg claimed in the *Star Trek* television series and one of the movies: resistance is futile. God and the God Self desire growth and change through experience. God is here to experience, not judge, control, punish, or reward.

The God Self and its objective for growth through new and different experiences, combined with its non-judgmental approach, is why evil and hatred exist. Though these behaviors are not the God Self's preference, and the God Self does not originate them, they, too, are experiences. It is our responsibility to choose to be good. Not for fear of punishment or to please God in exchange for favors, but because we strive to be in touch with the higher aspects within — in touch with the True Self, the God Self, and real Love. It is up to each of us to choose to exist within the energy of Love and to allow Love to influence and control our decisions and choices, rather than surrendering control to the Ego self and its fear-based version of reality.

When one transcends the Ego self and reaches the level of consciousness where Love becomes more motivating than fear, it then becomes possible to exist and experience life purely from the perspective of the True Self and Love. Even after attaining this higher state of being, though, staying in that state will never be automatic. To remain there, a conscious choice must be made continually, moment-to-moment, day after day. Attaining and maintaining that state, though, does enable the God Self to express itself through you, and to the world.

Your God Self is connected to and is part of the Greater God — the entirety of the universe — just like single molecule of water is part of the ocean. Your God Self compiles experiences and the wisdom gained is automatically added to the Greater God, becoming part of the consciousness of all. Everything is recorded and added to consciousness. Nothing falls through the cracks. Everything becomes part of the language and knowledge of the universe, thus continuing the expansion and evolution of God and consciousness.

Since all are connected to the Greater God, all are connected to one another as well as to the plants, trees, animals, and more. This holds true even if you don't yet have awareness of your God Self or your connection to these things. It is your choice to expand your awareness to include these treasures. Everything is one. Everything is in you, and you are in everything. The God Self knows this, and now you do, too.

10

The Communicator

Now, let's move to a more complete discussion about the Communicator. For convenience and simplicity, I have referred to the Communicator as one of the Inner Selves. In reality, the Communicator is more a tool, a conduit to be used by the Inner Selves, than it is a Self. It is, however, an extremely powerful, important, and useful component of your inner architecture.

Free will and choice have been mentioned numerous times throughout this book. This is a critical aspect of our existence, offering the option to shape our lives as we would like them to be. I've also discussed the Individualized Self in great detail. Our tastes, preferences, desires, dreams, and how we view and experience our physical existence all are contained in this aspect of us.

Due to the influence of the Ego self, the Individualized Self tends to identify with the physical body and the brain (which we must remember is separate from the mind). However, God is also part of who we are. We all have a God Self inside. These two major components, the Individualized Self and the God Self, though always connected, are kept at arm's length from one another. The Communicator is the medium between the God Self and the Individualized Self and is necessary to assure and maintain our gift of free will and choice. It allows communication without interference or obligation.

There are a couple of questions that may come to mind: Since we have the God Self inside of us, why does the Individualized Self make our choices, and not the God Self? Why doesn't the God Self dominate our thinking and actions? The answers are revealed in the fundamental catalyst for growth and higher consciousness: experience.

At birth, we're each given the ability to control our lives, just like a pilot controls a plane. We're blessed with the power to chart our own path; to pick and choose the experiences we'd like to have and the things we'd like to create. And we are free to create and experience anything and everything we desire, even if some or all of these things are considered bad or evil, and are contrary to the pursuit of higher consciousness. We're allowed to make mistakes. That's how we learn.

The primary purpose of life is to experience our world and grow from the experiences. Anything else, even those things which may be believed to be a purpose, is secondary, and likely not a true purpose at all. It is through these very experiences that consciousness itself, the Greater God, continually expands. And, much to our delight, it does this without judging us. Therefore, it is up to each of us to make our own choices, and to choose responsibly — to be kind, considerate, and to respect the Golden Rule (defined below) — but also to accept the consequences of our choices, good and bad. We are allowed to choose, create, and experience the negative or positive side of life, regardless of who we may hurt or help along the way. The choices we make today, however, will influence the experiences and options that come our way in the future.

The gift of free will and choice dictates that the Individualized Self chooses our experiences. The Individualized Self exists for eternity, but in our physical world is made complete with the addition of the Ego self at the time of birth, when we incarnate into a physical body. The Ego self is the aspect of ourselves that enables a fuller experience of the three-dimensional world we inhabit, but it is not intended to be the designated driver in this world. The intention and goal is that it operate in conjunction with the True Self to create a more holistic Individualized Self and a balanced approach as we create the life we'd like to live. Unfortunately, this is not the way things work out for almost everyone.

The Ego self, in one form or another, and to a greater or lesser degree depending on one's level of consciousness, takes a more dominant role. It often overpowers the True Self to take control of the Individualized Self and, thus, controls most of our choices and experiences. Additionally, the Ego self is pressured and influenced to make many of these choices by one's familial status and situation, as well as the socioeconomic and environmental realities. Add to this a more abstract factor: Our choices might also be influenced by past lifetimes, even when memories of past lives may not be conscious or easily accessible. They are part of us and can influence our current lives. All these things, and more, contribute to the choices we make as we go through life and can make them confusing and difficult. But they don't have to be.

This is free will and choice in action. We get to choose who we want to be, what we want to experience, how we react to outside stimuli, and what we want to create and add to the world. Of course, the choices we make shape our experiences, both good and bad, and the poor choices may have some uncomfortable consequences. These are not punishments, even when they seem so. And if we involve others in our choices, especially if they have not consented to participate, the consequences can be even more problematic. So, it is wise to make choices that do not violate what I believe should be the Golden Rule, which may be somewhat different from what you've previously learned. In my view it should not be about "Doing unto others…" as we've all heard. Instead, it would be more useful think about the Golden Rule as: "Do not involve anyone else in your life and your choices unless and until you have their prior permission to do so." Anything short of this creates a karmic debt which will have to be paid at some time in the future. These debts can, and often do, follow you into future lives.

Now, you may be thinking, "Ok, so we have free will. Great. But you also said we are God, that we have a God Self within. How is it possible that this God Self is separate from this all-important decision-making process? And, why would it allow us to create evil and cause pain to others?"

These questions get right to the heart of the of our Spiritual nature and the function of the Communicator. The answer to the second question about evil and pain comes down to this: There is no judgment. The God Self does not judge, it only experiences. To facilitate the accumulation of experience, it will assist in creating whatever the Individualized Self decides and properly communicates.

As to the first question about separation, this is where the Communicator plays a vital role. If the God Self forced its ideals on us, would we really have free will and choice? If we had no choice but to choose only what the God Self wanted, would that be the same as allowing us to choose the life we wanted to live, to experience the things we desire? Would that really be free will, or would that be coercion, a controlling force determining how we behave?

If we were punished for choices that differ from the ideals and Love of the God Self, there would be no free will. We would be controlled, and therefore not free to make our own choices. Like a puppet on a string, we would be forced to choose according to the wishes and desires of a puppet master, or suffer dire consequences. This is not free will and self-determination. It is control through vengeance and, contrary to some religious beliefs, God and the God Self are not vengeful. Vengeance is the opposite of Love and its basic tenet: allowing.

To not have free will would diminish the need and function of the Individualized Self. It would be the same as telling a child to go out and play any game they'd like. But if the child chose tag rather than hide-and-seek, they would be punished — sent to their room without any supper. God does not operate that way. It does not evaluate your choices. It allows them, honors them, and will help you create and achieve them, whatever they are, good or bad, without judgment.

With that in mind, let us now discuss the role of the Communicator.

The Communicator is a buffer between the Individualized Self and the God Self. This buffer assures a separation of powers. It's a safeguard to guarantee free will and choice by keeping a distance between these two inner aspects of you. It's a barrier that also facilitates communications between them but these are mostly one-way, usually from the Individualized Self to the God Self. It is rarely used by the God Self to convey messages in the opposite direction.

The God Self freely gives advice and guidance, but only when it is asked directly and specifically for this information. As the saying goes: "Ask and you shall receive." Answers and communications from the God Self are transmitted to us in various ways, but rarely through the Communicator. These might come in the form of an internal voice or a strong feeling which, when fully examined and explored, might bring thoughts or visualizations with the answers. But the God Self will never impose its desires on us, as this is contrary to its gift of free will and choice and would subvert the Communicator's purpose.

To hear communications from the God Self, one must be tuned to their inner world and the Inner Selves. Think of these communications like radio transmissions. A radio must be tuned to a specific channel or frequency to hear the desired program. Most people do not hear the inner guidance of the God Self because they are too busy creating and chasing the many distractions mentioned throughout this book. In other words, they're tuned to the wrong channel. When this is the case, we're more likely to hear the static that drowns out the quiet and subtle communications from the God Self.

Those already living in the highest realms of consciousness may receive guidance and answers or other communications from the God Self via the Communicator. Due to their higher level of conscious existence, they are better able to recognize or *hear* these communications and would better be able to contextualize them. They would not feel coerced and would still be able to allow their Individualized Self to make their choices.

The rest of us, those existing at levels of consciousness not quite as high, do not experience this. These communications would be too subtle for us, so we'd likely miss them or possibly perceive them as directives, rather than answers or suggestions. So, the God Self refrains from using the Communicator to send messages to us, though it regularly receives the messages we knowingly or unknowingly send to it through the Communicator. Rather, it uses other inner-world methods to speak to us, such as feelings within the body.

It is important to note that unless we ask a specific question explicitly directed to our God Self, the God Self will remain silent, in the background. It will not impose or intercede in our life and choices, with one minor exception. There are times when the God Self may "nudge" us in a direction through a gentle suggestion, also likely in the form of a feeling. This only happens when the suggestion — not an order — is in accordance with the plan we'd created for ourselves before being born into the current life, and the time has come to implement that part of the plan. It's still up to us to accept the nudge or ignore it. Once we are here in the physical realm we are free to deviate from that original plan, though that's usually not wise. If karma is involved, the ignored issue will have to be addressed at some point, either later in this lifetime or in another, and the longer we wait, the more challenging it may be.

The God Self doesn't judge our choices, even when they are contrary to its suggestions. And it will never punish us for them. The God Self simply acts on our behalf to help us create whatever we desire.

Consciously using the Communicator does require mastering a certain technique. Even though the Communicator is a direct line to our God Self, not everything we think or desire is automatically transmitted through it. To use this channel to communicate, we must be focused emotionally and intellectually; have a clear, balanced, and quiet brain; and we must generate and sustain strong feelings. Love or gratitude are preferred feelings for this purpose, but we are not limited to these. Any feelings will work to open the Communicator. Feelings are the keys that open this door and generate a current to carry your desires to the God Self. A genuine feeling must be present in the body, combined with your desire, to properly convey your desire through the Communicator and to the God Self. The desire can be sent by holding an image of the desire in the mind's eye, or as a worded thought. This technique is needed so that the God Self recognizes that we are making a serious request, and not just daydreaming. Then, if we are consistent, the God Self will go to work to help us create our desire, regardless of whether it is good or bad.

Since the God Self is likely to communicate back to us through feelings within the body, internal awareness is needed to make all this work. This is how most people will hear the voice of their God Self. Those who are more advanced and have already made a deeper connection with the God Self will eventually hear an internal voice, but it will only answer you when questioned. Otherwise, it will be silent. Like most things, learning to hear this internal voice is a skill that anyone can develop. But to avoid doubts or confusion, feelings can always confirm what has been heard or otherwise received.

Here's another item to consider: All this works whether you want it to, or not, which can create unintended consequences. Many people have not developed the ability to consciously control their thoughts and feelings. Not all thoughts need to be controlled, but it is important to be aware when you are obsessing about something. The adage that seems most appropriate is "Be careful what you wish for." Even though you don't really want some things to happen, if you stress about these things — imagine them over and over in your mind — it is likely that you will also create an internal, emotional energy, possibly the energy of fear. Even if this energy is subtle and you are not consciously aware of its internal presence, fear is a strong feeling and it will open the Communicator. If this happens, everything's in place — both the thought and the emotional energy needed to open and propel the thought through the Communicator, and directly to the God Self. If these are reinforced by repeating this pattern, the God Self will consider it to be a desire and will set out to create this experience for you, even though it's not what you really want.

For example: Imagine worrying about your financial situation, fearing that you will not have enough money or will lose money in an investment. If you spend too much time thinking about this, and frequently get emotional about it (create some fear within, even if you aren't aware of this inner feeling), you are using the Communicator to send this message to the God Self. Rather than evaluate the wisdom of this request, it will comply, creating an environment and situation for this to manifest in your life. Soon, in the absence of contrary thoughts also properly transmitted through the Communicator, you might find yourself in an unwanted financial quagmire.

Although you may not have intended it, you actually created it. This is why it is helpful and important to monitor and become aware of the thoughts and feelings within your body, and to spend more time thinking about the things you desire, while doing your best to avoid thinking about things you do not want to manifest in your life. You may have heard the term "Law of Attraction." The Law of Attraction is a real thing, and this is how that process works. Be aware of your Communicator and its job of transmitting your desires to your God Self for creation. You are a co-creator with your God Self.

Many people try affirmations to improve their lives. Many find that affirmations do not work. One possible reason is they are not using the Communicator. Affirmations can help but have a greater likelihood of working when the Communicator is used as part of the process. Proper use of the Communicator to transmit the affirmation to the God Self will give affirmations an added boost of power.

Before doing affirmations, open the Communicator by creating some internal energy, especially internal feelings in the heart. Think about joy or gratitude or Love. Get into the thought so that you feel the emotion generate within your body. Then move that energy — simply visualize it moving — to the heart area within your chest. Hold that feeling for a few seconds and *voila!*, the Communicator is now open and ready to transmit the gist of your affirmations directly to your God Self. The channel through the Communicator will remain open for a few minutes and will then close, unless you continue to generate additional internal feelings.

The Communicator is a valuable tool. It's importance and power in our lives can be arbitrary or directed. Will you consciously use it to create the things you'd like to experience in your life? Or will you remain asleep, unaware of your thoughts and feelings, and allow your Ego self to create your experiences based only on fear? The choice is yours.

11

Life after Death

I n an effort to keep everything suitably light-hearted, let's move to a discussion about death. Just kidding. The thought of death causes fear for many. Others are more curious about it, especially those who believe or know that death isn't the end. These people look forward to the next phase of life's wonderful cycle, whatever it may be.

Is there life after death? Is there a heaven or a hell? Do we keep our individuality when we die? Do we reincarnate? In this chapter, I will offer my perspective as I attempt to answer these questions (some directly and some indirectly).

My opinions about death are based on my real-world experiences in this life, and the wisdom I've gained throughout my years of relentless introspective, Spiritual self-examination. Even though my ideas about death are grounded in things I know are real it is not possible for me to actually *prove* them. As such, I readily accept that some readers may not be convinced that my observations regarding death are correct. Some will want more proof and that's okay. Skepticism and questioning are worthy paths to understanding and finding the wisdom within.

Each person will reach their own understanding of both life and death in their own time. For some, there is nothing I can say to convince them that there is more to us after we die. Others, upon reading this, may feel a spark within — an awakening, perhaps — and/or a sudden feeling of warmth or comfort. If you experience any of these sensations, (feelings), consider it your God Self communicating with you to take notice, that the words you are reading here are true.

From my 20s right through my 40s, I feared death. The inevitability of death, and being unaware of when it would come, were horrible thoughts as they crossed my mind. I used to count the years I might have had left, assuming my lifespan would be average for men living in the USA during the 1980s, which was about 73 years back then. (Since, it has increased and, given my familial genes and the Spiritual wisdom I have been blessed with, my current expectation is much higher.) With each passing day, though, time continued its onward march, as it does, rapidly taking those remaining days from the imaginary reserve I'd created for myself. Once these years had finished, due to my advances in consciousness, my fear of death abated.

As an aside, it is unfortunate that our limited sense of reality denies us the ability to fully manipulate time which, interestingly, science has suggested doesn't really exist. Nevertheless, in our physical world, we've yet to bring this observation to fruition so, naturally, many of us take steps to extend our time here. We take care of the body with exercise, healthy eating, and the wise among us add inner Spiritual work, like the sort I suggest in this book, and more. When we're calm, balanced, and in touch with our Inner Selves, including the God Self, the tendency is to take appropriate actions to be healthier and happier. We become less stressed. These things tend to extend one's physical years. Plus, since we have the God Self within, the body is the actual temple of God, so keeping its house in good and healthy order seems an appropriate form of worship.

In addition to increases in consciousness, I have been blessed with sporadic memories of some past life experiences. These certainly contributed to my growing comfort with life and death, as did my intellectual acceptance that there's little that can be done to avoid this inevitability. But what really convinced me and brought things into greater focus was a life-altering event I experienced during this lifetime.

On October 15, 2015, I was out on my daily bike ride. Early on in my Spiritual journey I found that aerobic exercise like running and cycling helped me reach a state during which I am able to connect with the deepest parts of myself.

On this particular day, shortly after beginning my ride — only about two blocks from my house on a wide road with plenty of room for bikes and motor vehicles to share — a car travelling at about forty-five miles per hour smashed into me from behind.

Now, I specifically chose to ride in this area because it was relatively safe. Safety is always a concern when cycling, but especially in Tampa, Florida. The Tampa area has a notorious and well-deserved reputation as the death capital of the world for cyclists. Everyone I know who cycles here has had at least one problem with an automotive vehicle, most of these accidental, but some not.

What made this experience even more strange was, prior to being hit, I had sensed danger without seeing or hearing anything overtly threatening. I was looking straight ahead as the wind whistled past my ears, drowning out all other sounds.

I had a subtle feeling urging me to increase my speed, to get out of the way, but drastically increasing my speed at that point in my ride was not something I'd normally do. I was still warming up. But I followed the instinct and did increase my speed from fifteen miles an hour to twenty. About six months after being hit, I found the courage to look at the data from my bike computer and confirmed this increase.

That's the last thing I remember. According to witnesses, once I was hit, my body flipped over the car, shattering both the front and back windshields, and then flew through the air before crashing onto the rough, asphalt road. My bike kept going forward. The bike computer's GPS showed that the speed of my bike had increased substantially on impact. In less than one second, the GPS registered an increase from twenty miles per hour to thirty-eight miles per hour. Applying the concept of kinetic energy to this information, and accounting for any increase in speed being diminished due to my bike shoes being clipped to the pedals — the bike went one way, I went the other, and the act of the shoes disconnecting from the bike diminished the bike's increasing speed as it hurtled through the air — the car was going an estimated forty-five miles per hour when it hit me, maybe more.

The driver didn't stop. He was a troubled young man who left me to die. According to the police who investigated the accident, he was unfamiliar with that neighborhood and got lost. He was also found to have the drug Spice in his system, and maybe others. As he drove the area looking for his escape route, he came upon some people on a side street only two short blocks away from our home. He stopped and asked them for directions, mentioned

the accident, and asked them to call 911. It is unclear why he
didn't call 911 himself, as he did have a phone. I was told he had
blood on his hands and, his car, a silver Lincoln MKZ, was badly
damaged. Maybe he was in shock.

The people called 911 immediately. (Many months later, I
sought out those caring folks and thanked them.) They also told
the driver that he should return to the scene of the accident as it
is a felony in Florida for a driver to leave an accident involving
bodily injury. He ignored that advice and drove off, leaving the
area. Later that day, he committed suicide. He purposely drove
his car headfirst into an oncoming emergency vehicle that was
responding to another accident, one completely unrelated to my
situation.

Now, here's the aspect of this experience which helped me
overcome any lingering skepticism I'd had about life after death.
As you might imagine, I was hospitalized with many broken bones
— there were more than ten, spanning my entire body, literally
from head to toe — including two broken vertebrae, a displaced
fracture of the femur in my right leg, and other severe injuries.
During the beginning weeks of hospitalization, I was conscious
and talking. I was lucid and able to give my wife important information about things she needed to do to keep my businesses
running smoothly. But the real me simply wasn't there. I have no
recollection or awareness of this time, even though I was awake
and lucid and I'd had many logical conversations with friends and
family members.

But there's a more interesting factor. About two weeks after
being hospitalized, I was acutely aware of the moment when I
returned to my physical body. By this time, I'd had two major
surgeries, was out of intensive care, and in a semi-private room.
I was alone, laying in my hospital bed, an awareness that only
became apparent after the following process had occurred. A

strange sensation began filling my body and my vision seemed to change. Like a dark fog fading away, the room and my surroundings suddenly came into focus, like a scene in a movie fading from dark to light. At that moment I had reentered my body; my awareness came back.

It took several months for me to bring together all the pieces of this puzzle. When I did, I realized that although I'd been awake and speaking during the initial weeks of hospitalization, most of me was not in my body. There was enough of me there, likely the Ego self and a small portion of my God Self, to keep the body going and to speak. Other parts of *me*, of the *Individualized Self* — my True Self — and perhaps the rest of my God Self, weren't fully within my body until that moment when I'd witnessed the fog as it lifted and my awareness returned.

I now know that the real me was somewhere else, outside of my body taking care of other things. Until the day I returned to it, I have no memories of the friends who'd visited — even though we had conversations and I apparently enjoyed their company — nor do I remember anything we discussed. However, after I saw the room open up as I returned to my body, my memories have been complete and vivid.

So, where was I during that time? I cannot say for certain. By design, I have no memory of that, either. I say "by design" as I believe that had I been given a more conscious understanding of my activities and experiences while I was away from my body, I might not have returned. It is possible, even likely, that my preference would have been a non-physical existence and I would have chosen to remain there. But it was not my time to stay in that place. There was more for me to do on this plane of existence, the physical world.

In fact, it seems that my path specifically called for me to not only live, but also to not be paralyzed. Two of my doctors used the word "miracle" to describe my injuries and prognosis for re-covery. I'd broken my back in two different places: a burst fracture of T-4, and a compression fracture of L-1. The most critical was the fracture to T-4. I now have a massive titanium structure in my back, extending from T-2 to T-6, which was implanted to keep my back secure while it healed. Immediately after the procedure, the doctor who surgically installed that hardware commented to my wife that it was miraculous that there had been no spinal cord damage, saying he'd never seen an injury like it that didn't also include spinal cord damage. He thought that I should have been paralyzed to some degree, but I wasn't. In fact, I recovered so fully that, in addition to riding my bike, I can do everything I'd like, including skiing on the beautiful snow in the Rocky Mountains.

Another major injury I'd suffered was the one to the femur in my right leg. It was fractured close to my hip and completely dis-placed. The orthopedic surgeon who'd repaired that injury, which required another ample portion of titanium rods and screws, also used the word "miracle." (I've been told that doctors don't usually use that word, but according to the notes taken by my wife during that difficult time, it was used twice about me by those two differ-ent doctors.) His use of the term, though, was a bit more ominous than the neurosurgeon's. He told my wife that once he'd opened up my hip and saw all the soft tissue damage in the area, he thought it was a miracle that I had not bled out and died.

The point of including the above details about this accident is not to elicit sympathy but to share information about the like-lihood that a force beyond our basic understanding, perhaps my God Self, had interceded on my behalf, allowing me to continue living and to do so with full mobility. Additionally, it is interesting that I have no recollection of the pain one might associate with these many injuries. I had many other broken bones from this ac-cident, some very serious, and some less so, but my recollection of

the pain suffered is minimal when compared to the reasonable expectations of pain associated with these sorts of injuries. It doesn't
mean that pain was not there. It's just that it is not part of my
awareness and, thus, my experience. This seems significant as only
the day before the accident during a conversation with my God
Self, I had asked for some assistance in the healing of my body.
The only request I added was: please no pain. The injuries I suffered during this accident did actually contribute to the healing of
those other issues, those with which I had requested help. Seems
like a validation of the phrase, "careful what you wish for"!

So, what really happened during the time when I was awake
and communicating but had no awareness of myself or my surroundings? Some might say that I'd just lost consciousness.
Possibly, but how can that be if I was awake and able to have
complete, lucid conversations with others, even directing my wife
where to find things in my office, and telling her the things which
needed to be done to keep the businesses going? Others might say
that I was in shock. Also possible, but for several weeks when I was
able to have cogent and intellectual conversations? Additionally,
the medical team caring for me did not mention anything about
being in shock to my wife.

Consequently, to me, the most logical conclusion is that the
real *me* had left my body. Then, after completing whatever work
I'd been doing "on the other side" and after most of the pain
had subsided, I returned. I do understand if you are not similarly convinced but ask that you remain open to this possibility. In
a sense, this was a type of reincarnation. For me, it was enough
to validate the assertion that death — in the traditional sense —
doesn't exist. This validation was accompanied by a strong feeling
of experientially inspired, inner knowing. Experience is the way
wisdom is acquired. At the end of our physical existence, we just
leave the body and, depending on our particular path and plan,

can exchange it for a new one, reincarnate, or we can remain in the non-physical realms.

We don't just die. We just transition to a non-physical existence. And when we desire, we can return to another body. We're never forced to. We choose to. We always have free will and choice, even on the non-physical planes of existence.

So, take heart. You'll have more lives here on Earth if that's what you desire and choose. Or, you might want to experience and learn in a different place, in another physical world somewhere else in our universe. Either way, you're going to be alive for the long haul. Where you decide to go is up to you. You'll make that decision based on whatever is best for you at the time, whether it's another life on Earth, or an existence in another realm. And, your *individuality* will stay with you. You won't disappear into the vastness of all consciousness.

Here's what all this means: The real you does not, cannot, die. The real *you* is energy, the energy of consciousness. You are your God Self. And we all know from physics that energy cannot die, only transition. Therefore, neither the Greater God nor the God Self can die. If either did, everything would cease to exist since everything is God.

Additionally, I've been fortunate to have had my fair share of memories and visions from past lives, though some of these have been vague. I have not yet had visions of future lives which, according to science and its discussions about time, exist simultaneously. For me, these memories of past lives, along with the experience of the accident, completely validate the concept of re-incarnation. But there is something else; I've also had the joyful opportunity to hear from relatives and a friend on the other side, those who've passed away. They usually came to me during the day, while I was very much awake, rather than at night through a dream, and shared greetings and thoughts about how they were doing "on the other side." Each was doing very well and had been released from any psychological or physical pain they'd experienced during their last physical life. They were at peace.

12

What's Next

T he title of this book is *Discovering Your God Self... The Incredible Secrets of Your Spiritual Nature Revealed.* And, believe it or not, you now know everything you need to know — in basic terms, anyway — about the components of the real you and your Spiritual nature. Your soul encompasses five aspects, the Inner Selves, and this includes your God Self. There is much more to know — there's always more to know — including how to practically apply and use of this information, but that's beyond the scope of this book. This is the foundation of the physical/Spiritual blend that defines our human existence, and it is useful to understand this blend to help bring these inner elements into balance with themselves, with the physical body, and your experiences in the world.

You now have a quiver filled with powerful arrows of Spiritual knowledge. What do you do with this information? How can you use it to transform your life? As you continue forward on your path, wherever that may take you, please keep in mind that knowledge is not wisdom. Knowledge can be acquired through books, but wisdom is purely experiential. You cannot gain wisdom from books. The God Self is the source of wisdom and shares it through your connection with the True Self. Live your life and monitor your body and its feelings to become aware of your Inner Selves. When you do this, there will come a point when you become aware of your God Self. This connection is strengthened through the clearing away of unhealthy fears — debris — which, over time, have likely concealed the God Self from your awareness.

If you let it happen, acquired knowledge can lead to new and positive habits. Embrace the new knowledge you now have and make strides to acquire that all-important wisdom. Perhaps finishing this book has created some momentum for you. Keep it going. Pay closer attention to what is happening inside of you. Notice your inner world and the many ways it is expressed, either deliberately or unconsciously, in your outer world. Use this information to learn about yourself. Study yourself. Deep self-examination is the way forward. This will lead you to better decisions and more successful outcomes in all areas of life, from relationships and financial outcomes, to everything in between and beyond. Ultimately, you will experience an increase in contentment and happiness.

Learning about yourself will also give you insights into everything and everyone else. The more you know about your Inner Selves, the more you will know about others and the world you inhabit. At a Spiritual level, you and I are the same. We've just had different experiences which have shaped the way we view the world — the Individualized Self — and have guided the actions we take.

Here are two things I recommend you do:

1. Make a conscious effort to become aware of your Inner Selves. Don't be distracted by everything going on outside of you. Understand it is more important to focus on what's inside of you, because that's where everything real takes place. As much as is possible, place your focus there. (Note: This does not mean to only focus there. For example: It's not a good idea to be completely focused internally when driving a car. We have the senses for good reason.) To do this, you must allow yourself the privilege of feeling. Be continually aware of how your body is feeling in any given moment. Know that your body is a communicating tool and will give you the necessary information if you pay attention.

2. Meditation is a valuable tool to help you uncover your Inner Selves. It will help you raise your consciousness. But know that meditation is not the endpoint of this journey. It is only a tool for you to use to help you find your way. There are many types of meditation. Don't concern yourself with finding the best practice, especially if you are just starting out. The important thing is to try to do it every day so you can eventually discover the method that works best for you.

If you miss a day, have no fear. Your Inner Selves aren't going anywhere. They'll always be there and will be just fine if anything distracts you from meditation for a day, a week, a month, or even years. If this happens, just bring yourself back and get going again. Consistent meditation leads to changes in the structure of the brain. The more you do it, the more it will change for the better!

a.   *If you'd like to learn some of the techniques I have used during meditation, I created a web page with information and videos about breathing exercises to help contact the God Self—feel its presence within—and visualization techniques that can help quiet your mind and bring your focus inward. Here's a link directly to that page: https:// brucebernstein.me/extras-discovering-your-god-self/*

Let your new habits form naturally and try not to force things that are uncomfortable in that moment. If they're truly needed, their day will come. But don't give up, either. Allow yourself the luxury of time to adjust and become comfortable with these things.

Developing awareness of the physical sensations within your body is the best place to begin. There may be times when you will feel sensations in your chest or solar plexus area. Or maybe you'll feel anger emerging and flowing upwards from the base of your spine. These physical sensations may have crucial messages for you. Those that seem disruptive or uncomfortable will express discord at some level within. The next time you become aware of these sorts of feelings, allow yourself to feel them and their discomfort. Acknowledge them with Love. Ignoring or attempting to push them aside will only give the underlying cause more power for future disruptions in your life.

These uncomfortable feelings will dissipate and release if you let them. Show them respect and Love. Communicate with them. Speak directly to them. Ask them to tell you why they are there. Listen for the response. They will answer and you will hear if you are listening. Feeling, acknowledging, and then communicating with them as you would a young child who is learning from mistakes is an immensely powerful technique of release. And release is necessary to uncover the gold already there, buried within — the God Self. This is how to build a bridge back to your source.

Similarly, allow, feel, and listen for any messages from the calmer and more comfortable feelings that emerge within you. These also have crucial things to tell you.

Many times, your feelings are communications from your Inner Selves. Discomfort, disappointment, and fear are all feelings generated by your Ego self. These can take the form of butterflies in the stomach, or general nervousness, or even sensations of temperature fluctuations like warmth or cold. Learn to recognize and feel them from the moment they first bubble up within your body. And please remember, when I say feelings, I'm not talking about an intellectual process such as the statement "You hurt my feelings," which usually is a *thinking* reaction to something someone else has said or done.

Sure, there are times when others will say things that generate internal feelings. But these feelings always are ours — self-generated. They are not something the other person created within you. Feelings are our own creations and it is our responsibility to address them. They will reveal answers to questions you may have about the many aspects of your life, such as happiness, Love, success, and more. And if someone says or does something that elicits an uncomfortable or displeasing feeling response within — in other words, they "hurt you" — it is helpful to recognize that these feelings likely are coming from your Ego self. This is not to say that unhealthy or abusive relationships should be allowed to continue unabated. You are always in charge. You can and should take action to change unwanted experiences. But your True Self does not become hurt by what others say or do, nor does the God

Self. There is no judgment there and judgment is required to feel emotional pain. Only the Ego self judges. It is the center of any emotional pain you feel.

Just as you have feelings emanating from your Ego self, you also have feelings generated by your True Self. Love, allowing, trust, compassion, and empathy are feelings that sprout from your True Self. You should feel these, too. They will have a decidedly different feel from those generated by the Ego self. These usually will be the more calm, comfortable, and warm feelings.

Becoming self-aware is all about the process of learning about your Inner Selves. Feelings are things that everyone has, regardless of where they may be along their path to higher consciousness, and these feelings — if given the appropriate attention described above — will lead to wisdom and the continued expansion of your awareness of your Spiritual nature. It's all too easy to turn these feelings off. This is what too many people do, usually as a defense mechanism against things that bring inner discomfort or "hurt." This is a mistake. Instead, it is more useful to address these diffi- cult feelings courageously. Bring them into your conscious aware- ness, into the light, and soothe their pain with Love.

Let yourself feel. Of course, you will experience feelings that will be uncomfortable at times, and memories that have been buried in various places within your body may come to the surface; make themselves known. This is a good thing, even if it doesn't feel good at the time. All these feelings need to be pro- cessed, cleared, and released for you to uncover your God Self within. This is how you clear away the debris that's been keeping you from realizing and accessing this powerful source of energy and wisdom. The technique to process these things, to let them go, is one of Love. The word "let" is used aptly, meaning we have to allow them to leave. Too many of us develop an attachment to these things — we hold onto them — keeping them in place due to the comfort we have developed with the pain they produce. We must *let* them leave through acknowledgement, encouragement, and Love.

Treat your inner feelings of hurt and anger this way. This is how to process and let go of your Ego self's fears and the fear-based, outer world actions and reactions they generate.

One thing I want to say as you near completion of this book: congratulations! You have made important strides in your journey. As you proceed along your path, it should become easier than you might think, as long as you choose easy rather than difficult. Let yourself feel and become consciously aware of your feelings. Tear down the walls of energy that stand between you, your Individualized Self, and your God Self. This is how you will find your God.

Start by monitoring your body and notice how and what you are feeling. These can be comfortable or uncomfortable feelings. It doesn't matter. Let yourself feel them, no matter what they are. Then learn to discern between those generated by the Ego self and those coming from the True Self. This is the key to making better choices. This, more than anything else, will be the greatest help in your decision-making. If your God Self is communicating with you through your feelings, you will want to hear what it has to say.

Open your heart and find your God Self. Hear this powerful, inner voice of truth and Love. It's all up to you. Take action. Use what you have learned to discover your God Self.

And here's a little bonus. Everyone I have ever encountered wants to talk to God. But even more, they want to hear God talking to them.

The information you now have is the foundation needed to hear the voice of your God — the God Self within — when it speaks to you. And it does speak to you. Are you listening?

Afterward

Discovering Your God Self... The Incredible Secrets of Your Spiritual Nature Revealed took much longer to write than I had anticipated. Some of the delays were a product of the sorts of worldly distractions I've written about on the preceding pages. One, which was completely unrelated to the book, was something my wife and I created. We sold our home of many years in the midst of a very active real estate market. Subsequently, we struggled to find an acceptable, new place to live. Homes were selling within hours of being listed for sale — literally hours. Due to this unnatural real estate activity, mostly created by the Covid 19 pandemic, the search for a new home took months longer than anticipated. This devoured much time and the emotional energy needed for me to draw the information from within and cogently scribble them onto these pages.

There was more. During one of my bike rides, my God Self confessed that it had also contributed to the delays. In addition to creating other distractions to grab my attention and blur my focus — many of these were the normal daily things that seemingly crop up in life — it also made good use of the scenario my wife and I had created when we sold our old home. Beyond the highly unusual market activity, other things happened that were outside our control that lengthened the time it took for us to find and buy a new place. I learned during that particular ride that all these things were intended to keep me distracted and not working on the book.

The reason for this sabotage, and I use that term in an affectionate way, was that I did not yet have all the information needed to complete this book. During the delays, information continued to filter through the ethers and into my conscious awareness so that it could be included in the preceding chapters. Often, this information first presented itself during my bike rides but came more into focus sometime later, usually as my fingers danced across the keyboard to include it herein.

Notwithstanding the confusing relationship I've always had with vigorous exercise, the bike rides have been, and remain a critical component of my Spiritual growth and increased consciousness. Growth in consciousness is a never-ending process. It is accomplished through diligent pursuit using the acquired skills of deepening awareness. It is not something that is *gained*. Rather, it is a process of *allowing*. It simply emerges through intense and honest self-exploration.

Don't stop, regardless of the distractions, both inner and outer world, which undoubtedly will come your way. These will pass. Then, bring your focus back to the bigger goal.

Made in the USA
Las Vegas, NV
10 April 2024

88508463R00090